I0048094

Assessing Canada's System of Impact Evaluation of Active Labour Market Policies

OECD))

BETTER POLICIES FOR BETTER LIVES

This work is published under the responsibility of the Secretary-General of the OECD. The opinions expressed and arguments employed herein do not necessarily reflect the official views of the Member countries of the OECD.

This document, as well as any data and map included herein, are without prejudice to the status of or sovereignty over any territory, to the delimitation of international frontiers and boundaries and to the name of any territory, city or area.

The statistical data for Israel are supplied by and under the responsibility of the relevant Israeli authorities. The use of such data by the OECD is without prejudice to the status of the Golan Heights, East Jerusalem and Israeli settlements in the West Bank under the terms of international law.

Please cite this publication as:
OECD (2022), *Assessing Canada's System of Impact Evaluation of Active Labour Market Policies*, Connecting People with Jobs, OECD Publishing, Paris, https://doi.org/10.1787/27dfbd5f-en.

ISBN 978-92-64-39384-4 (print)
ISBN 978-92-64-32011-6 (pdf)

Connecting People with Jobs
ISSN 2616-4132 (print)
ISSN 2616-4140 (online)

Foreword

Giving people better opportunities to participate in the labour market is a key policy objective in all OECD and EU countries. Better employment increases disposable income, strengthens economic growth and improves well-being. Well-tailored labour market and social protection policies are a key factor in the creation of high-quality jobs and increasing the number of people looking for work. Policies need to address pressing structural challenges, such as rapid population ageing and evolving skill needs, including those needed for the green transition. They should also foster social inclusion and mobilise all of society.

The COVID-19 pandemic has increased the need for policies to support employment and inclusive labour markets. Even before the crisis, employment rates differed markedly across population groups. High unemployment, weak labour market attachment of some population groups and unstable or poor-quality employment reflect a range of barriers to working or moving up the jobs ladder. The economic repercussions of the pandemic risk entrenching these barriers further. It will be a major challenge for policy makers in the coming years to lift these labour market obstacles, support labour relocation and make labour market participation accessible for all.

Another challenge that policy makers face is the effective and efficient use of public funds. Knowing what policies work is critical and this requires collecting relevant data, careful planning of impact evaluations and use of their results to guide policy making. Advances in data collection and storage and modern computer power means that countries now have a greater ability than ever before to conduct evaluations of their policies using high-quality administrative data and survey data. Expertise is needed to take these data and conduct robust and credible policy evaluation. Communication of their results is vital to inform policy makers.

The OECD Employment, Labour and Social Affairs Committee is carrying out a set of reviews of labour market and social protection policies to encourage greater labour market participation and better employment among all population groups with a special focus on the most disadvantaged who face the greatest barriers to finding quality jobs. This includes a series of country studies, *Connecting People with Jobs*, which provide an assessment of how well active labour market policies (ALMPs) help all groups to move into productive and rewarding jobs, and a number of policy recommendations that could improve the situation. A number of reports in this series conduct impact evaluations of selected ALMPs and assess the systems countries have in place for evidence-informed policy making.

This report on Canada is the ninth country study published in this series. It focuses on how Canada leverages its administrative data to evaluate its ALMPs by examining how these evaluations are conducted, what methodologies are used, the quality assurance process and how results are communicated within the policy making process. This report, which is funded by Employment and Social Development Canada, forms part of a joint project by the OECD and the European Commission which aims to raise the quality of data collected on the outcomes and effectiveness of labour market programmes, so that countries can better evaluate and design them to benefit their citizens.

Acknowledgements

This report was prepared by Stewart Butler in the OECD's Directorate for Employment, Labour and Social Affairs, under the supervision of Theodora Xenogiani (project leader). Lucy Hulett provided editorial input. Dana Blumin provided statistical and editorial input.

The report would not have been possible without the input of colleagues in Canada. Staff in Employment and Social Development Canada inputted across a number of areas. Jérôme Mercier, Yves Gingras and Laura MacFadgen provided senior level input to support the project. Andy Handouyahia, Georges Awad and Essolaba Aouli provided their extensive expertise and organised a series of virtual fact-finding meetings with stakeholders. Policy, programme and data officials within ESDC have enriched the report with details on the evidence generation and policy making process within their organisation. Discussions with officials from British Colombia, New Brunswick, Newfoundland and Labrador, and Nova Scotia provided insights on the joint evaluation processes that take place between Provinces and Territories and ESDC and on delivery of active labour market policies within those areas. Large sections of the report are based on this engagement.

Thanks are also given to colleagues in the State Secretariat for Economic Affairs (SECO) in Switzerland and the Danish Agency for Labour Market and Recruitment (STAR) for providing insights about how their institutions use data to produce analysis of their labour market programmes. The report benefitted from discussions with Patrick Arni (University of Bristol) on the implementation of randomised control trials in Switzerland. Jeffrey Smith (University of Wisconsin-Madison) and Michael Lechner (University of St. Gallen, Swiss Institute for Empirical Economic Research) provided reflections on their work to provide ESDC advice on the outputs and methodology for the Labour Market Development Agreements evaluation.

Comments on earlier drafts of the report were provided by Stefano Scarpetta, Mark Keese, Sofia Dromundo and Judd Ormsby at the OECD.

Table of contents

FIGURES

TABLES

Follow OECD Publications on:

https://twitter.com/OECD

https://www.facebook.com/theOECD

https://www.linkedin.com/company/organisation-eco-cooperation-development-organisation-cooperation-developpement-eco/

https://www.youtube.com/user/OECDiLibrary

https://www.oecd.org/newsletters/

This book has...

StatLinks

A service that delivers Excel® files from the printed page!

Look for the *StatLink* at the bottom of the tables or graphs in this book. To download the matching Excel® spreadsheet, just type the link into your Internet browser or click on the link from the digital version.

Acronyms and abbreviations

ALMP	Active Labour Market Policy
APE	Action Plan Equivalent
ATT	Average treatment on treated
BFS	Swiss Federal Statistical Office (*Bundesamt für Statistik*)
CAD	Canadian Dollar
CASD	*Centre d'Accès Sécurisé aux Données (The Secure Access Data Center)*
CBA	Cost Benefit Analysis
CDO	Chief Data Office
CEM	Coarsened Exact Matching
CIE	Counterfactual Impact Evaluation
CPI	Consumer Price Inflation
CRA	Canada Revenue Agency
DID	Difference-in-difference
DWP	Department for Work and Pensions (United Kingdom)
EAS	Employment Assistance Services
EBSM	Employment Benefits and Support Measures
EI	employment insurance
ESDC	Employment and Social Development Canada (*Emploi et Développement social Canada*)
GDP	Gross Domestic Product
IAB	*Institut für Arbeitsmarkt*
IFAU	Institutet för arbetsmarknads- och utbildningspolitisk utvärdering (Institute for Evaluation of Labour Market and Education Policy)
ITT	Intention-to-treat
IV	Instrumental variables
JCP	Job Creation Partnerships
LMDA	Labour Market Development Agreements
LMPDP	Labour Market Programme Data Platform
LMTA	Labour Market Transfer Agreements
NZD	New Zealand Dollar
PISC	Privacy and Information Security Committee
PSM	Propensity Score Matching
PTs	Provinces and territories
RCTs	Randomised Control Trials
RDD	Regression Discontinuity Design
SD	Skills Development
SE	Self-Employment
TWS	Targeted Wage Subsidies
STAR	*Styrelsen for Arbejdsmarked og Rekruttering* (Danish Agency for Labour Market and Recruitment)
UI	Unemployment Insurance
USD	US Dollar
VfM	Value-for-money
WDAS	Workforce Development Agreements

Executive summary

Rigorous evaluation of public policies and programmes is a key step in informing policy making. Sound evidence on what works and for whom helps governments to achieve their strategic objectives. In recent years, the increasing availability of rich administrative data and computing power to conduct statistical analysis has meant that an increasing number of OECD countries are now able to conduct impact assessments of their policies using these rich data. Canada is an exemplar in this respect and the work of its employment and social affairs ministry, Employment and Social Development Canada (ESDC) in planning and conducting evaluation in collaboration with officials from Provinces and Territories (PTs) provides a good example of how to deliver such assessments. Knowing whether a policy is effective at achieving its stated aims and offers value for money is imperative to the sound utilisation of public funds and ESDC is now able to have fully informed discussions about its active labour market policy.

Prior to the pandemic, Canada's federal government invested around CAD 5 billion annually to deliver a range of active labour market policies (ALMP) to support individuals. The Labour Market Development Agreements (LMDA) – bilateral labour market transfers with provinces and territories – are the largest funding stream within this investment and the programmes that can be offered in it are defined in federal legislation. They span support and coaching for jobseekers to look for work, training to enhance skills, and recruitment subsidies and job creation to foster employment opportunities. There is further support for harder-to-help jobseekers financed separately through Workforce Development Agreements (WDAs), the second of the two labour market transfers to PTs. PTs may also supplement this funding with their own provincial programming. Altogether federal active labour market spending in 2019, excluding the WDAs, represented just over 0.2% of GDP, which placed Canada in the bottom half of spending among OECD countries. This share has been decreasing over time and was over 0.3% of GDP around the turn of the century. The LMDA have been flat in nominal terms since their introduction in 1996, with periodic top-ups of funding to meet demand. This goes some way to explaining the funding pressures on ALMPs over time in Canada, increasing further the importance of knowing what policies work and how effective they are, to ensure they are given adequate weighting in public finance debates.

Against this backdrop, **Canada has developed a highly proficient analytical capacity within ESDC to conduct policy evaluation of ALMPs**. Since the inception of the LMDA, there has been a transformation of both the process and delivery of policy evaluation. Funding was transferred to PTs with the requirement that they consult annually with labour market stakeholders in their respective jurisdictions and report back to ESDC on how those consultations inform their labour market priorities and programming. A legislative requirement was introduced for PTs to conduct regular evaluations of their policy delivery financed by the LMDA. All PTs except Quebec (which conducts its own evaluations) have chosen to discharge this responsibility through evaluations conducted jointly with ESDC. When these evaluations were first incarnated, they were delivered via external contractors and data was gathered via client surveys. This process was both costly, cumbersome and contained some inaccuracies in participants' recall of their income. It took around ten years for the first set of evaluations to be completed, as the nature of the surveys and associated analysis meant that only two to three studies could be conducted simultaneously.

ESDC embarked upon a programme of transformation, enlisting the use of administrative micro-data on employment insurance receipt and ALMP participation linked to Canada Revenue Agency data on income, and conducting analysis in-house. With strong provisions to protect personal information, ESDC has created a data platform from these separate datasets so that it can conduct assessments, this ensures consistency across evaluations of different policies and reduces data re-work for separate projects. ESDC has now conducted assessment of a number of different funding streams with these data. Increased internal resources for evaluation, due to lower contracting-out costs, and the establishment of a Chief Data Office have allowed ESDC to formalise and embed resources and best practice. ESDC is now able to deliver rigorous assessments of ALMPs, using established analytical techniques to ensure robustness, at a significantly quicker pace. These techniques are observational in nature, meaning linked administrative data are crucial in data processes which ensure that similar participants and non-participants are compared. These data also mean participants can also be sub-categorised so that effects for a range of different participants can be studied. A range of work is undertaken to assure the quality of this work, both to ensure the data and methods selected are appropriate and to test the sensitivity of estimates to various variations in these. ESDC has built a network of relationship with PTs officials and across analytical, data and programme staff within ESDC, using this teamwork to effectively deliver cycles of evaluation work. It also conducts a full cost benefit analysis of ALMPs, so that it can fully appraise them relative to one another. The utilisation of expert peer reviewers and the communication of analysis to external forums allows ESDC to ensure analysis is validated, fit-for-purpose, has credibility, and benefits from external analytical advice and expertise.

There are a number of small improvements that would further enhance ESDC's ability to conduct detailed impact assessment of its ALMPs.

- Enhancing some socio-economic data – such as education, family and immigration data – would allow better identification of sub-group impacts on young people, parents and migrants.

- Real-time access to tax records for income data would allow evaluations to be conducted two years earlier, allowing a more contemporaneous discussion of policy effectiveness.

- Conducting federal co-ordination of small-scale randomised studies within PTs, would allow more evidence to be gathered on programme delivery. PTs have considerable freedom in how they deliver programmes and their precise content, which introduces questions on delivery mode and programme design. For example, whether in-house delivery is more efficient than out-sourced, what the ideal contract design of out-sourced programmes is and what are optimal programme durations and content.

- Opening up ALMP data to external researchers, via Statistics Canada, would democratise and expand the range of analysis, permitting greater innovation, reducing the direct costs of analysis for ESDC and ensuring PTs can properly analyse their policy delivery.

- Breaking down the analysis that is used to estimate programme impacts into discrete stages would allow more discussion of how much the estimates change, and therefore how sensitive they are to their underlying assumptions.

- Considering weighting the outcomes for ALMP participants in cost-benefit analysis to recognise their low level of income on average relative to other Canadians, would allow ESDC to better position their funding requirements relative to other government ministries.

- Re-embedding the face-to-face forums for knowledge sharing between PTs after COVID-19 sanitary requirements have subsidised would allow for the continued fruitful exchange of analysis and policy delivery information between them.

1 Assessment and recommendations

Canada has invested significant time and resources to develop an advanced capacity in its employment ministry, Employment and Social Development Canada (ESDC), to undertake impact assessment of its active labour market policies (ALMPs). Its experience provides useful practical examples to countries on how to use data and deploy resources to generate evidence on programme effectiveness to support policy development. It utilises its rich administrative data on participation in ALMPs and incomes to underpin robust observational studies on programme effects. It undertakes these assessments internally, making use of expert external peer reviewers for quality assurance. Studies are published to document results, data and methodology and to communicate and contextualise results. Some improvements in both data and analytical techniques could further enrich the evidence base.

1.1. Canada offers a range of ALMPs to its citizens and evaluates their effectiveness

In 2019, prior to the pandemic, Canada's federal government invested around CAD 5 billion in its ALMPs to help individuals find work. For the largest funding stream ESDC, Canada's federal ministry with responsibility for employment insurance and ALMPs, transfers funding to the Provinces and Territories (PTs) through the Labour Market Transfers. These consist of Labour Market Development Agreements (LMDAs) and Workforce Development Agreements (WDAs). PTs are required under the transfers to consult annually with labour market stakeholders to inform labour market priorities and ensure that programming reflects local labour market conditions. Broad ALMP structures are laid down in federal legislation but the delivery of these programmes to individuals and the exact mix of programmes offered is devolved to the PTs. They enjoy flexibility in the mix of programmes delivered and how they are delivered; whether to deliver in-house or to externally contract, and if the latter how to design these contracts. There is a wide range of average costs of ALMPs by PTs, suggesting that this flexibility to tailor is something that happens in practice.

1.1.1. Canada offers a full range of ALMPs but there are some funding pressures

LMDAs provide eligible individuals with programmes such as skills training, recruitment and start-up subsidies, direct job creation and employment support services (including employment assistance services providing lighter touch interventions such as employment counselling, job search assistance and needs assessments). In 2019 these supported some 630 000 individuals to find work. However, despite the size and scale of this funding, spending as a percentage of GDP in Canada is still below the OECD average on both passive and active labour market measures and real spending per unemployed jobseeker in the decade to 2019 was some 22% lower than the decade to 2008. Of the programmes it offers, counselling services and training comprise the majority of the total volume. Relative to other OECD countries Canada has a strong focus on these in the basket of ALMPs it offers. Its job counselling services serve as a gateway to the extra programmes that are offered.

1.1.2. ALMP evaluation is cyclically mandated in legislation and jointly conducted by ESDC and 12 of the 13 PTs

When the LMDAs were established, they contained provisions to continuously evaluate the performance of ALMPs. This ensured that evidence-building was at the heart of policy delivery and facilitated ESDC to build a rich evidence base to support policy making. All but 1 of the 13 PTs opted to conduct these evaluations jointly with ESDC. The evaluations are conducted within cycles and presently ESDC is working on the third cycle of evaluation.[1] The first cycle took place between 1998 and 2012 and was completed on a bilateral basis with each of the participating 12 PTs- this limited the number of studies that could be run simultaneously. The second cycle, from 2012-17, augmented this arrangement, so that analysis was conducted simultaneously for all the PTs, allowing conclusions to be developed much more rapidly. The changes made between the first and second cycles (and now onto the third) provide insight into development to both data and processes that Canada has made in its evaluation of ALMPs.

1.1.3. ESDC evaluations show that ALMPs offer good value-for-money

An extensive evaluation of Canada's ALMPs has already been conducted, demonstrating that these programmes offer value for money to the taxpayer. This evaluation looks at a full suite of outcomes for individuals, including the impacts on income, employment insurance receipt and social assistance receipt. The work has shown that there are significant variations in programme impacts across both individuals and PTs, which may in part be related to the freedom that PTs have to design their programmes.

1.2. Impact evaluation of ALMPs required strong political will and strategic decisions

In Canada, at the federal level, each department is required to establish and maintain a robust, neutral evaluation function. In that context, ESDC has built a proficient evaluation directorate, which produces high-quality impact assessments of its ALMPs, replacing analysis that was previously contracted out. As ESDC demonstrated its ability to effectively implement evaluations in-house to a high standard and good timescales, it has been able to allocate greater resources to invest further in this area. This aligned with a shift around 2016 of the Canadian Government to focus much more on data, and place much more weight on its availability and use in policy evaluation.

1.2.1. ESDC made a decision to conduct evaluation work in-house

The choice over whether to deliver ALMP evaluations in-house or via external contractors is multi-faceted and countries employ different approaches, many opting for some combination. The choice of delivery mode is influenced by decision on the expertise needed to conduct the analysis, the possibility of making data available to external partners, the frequency of evaluation and the management of contractors and analytical narrative. Ministries with little or no analytical functions will be better placed to contract-out research.

There were a number of important elements to the successful shift towards a specialised in-house evaluation team in ESDC. Firstly, there was support and advocacy of the change internally in ESDC from senior leadership. Secondly, wider governmental level shift towards open data and evidence-based policy making provided broader support for the change. Thirdly, the presumption of cost savings generated a lot of goodwill – it had cost around CAD 1 million per annum to deliver the externally-commissioned survey-based analysis. The direct costs of external support were reduced to around CAD 70 000 per annum after the change. Even if this had to mean some internal diversion from previous analytical priorities, the optics of cost reduction can play an important element in guiding risk management and informing resource allocation within governmental organisations.

To support this, a core of analytical expertise with the requisite skills and motivation were built to support the transition. Dedicated resources for the evaluation of ALMPs were put in place. This was combined with a refocusing of other analytical capacity with an explicit mandate to manage the process of co-ordination with the PTs and to bring qualitative evidence to bear on the evaluations (vital to bring contextualise information to the analysis). Analytical expertise could now be devoted separately to data development, methodological work, qualitative research and project management. Crucial to this was the employment of expert external consultants to advise on methodology and outputs, providing credibility to the results and helping to lay down the initial framework for the evaluation and the data requirements.

1.2.2. ESDC has made changes to its organisation to reflect the importance of ALMP evaluations

ESDC's evaluation directorate is separated from the function that is responsible for ALMP development and implementation. The branch where the evaluation directorate sits has responsibility for the strategic management of data, for programme evaluation and for intergovernmental and international relations. It contains the evaluation directorate, which conducts all of the counterfactual impact evaluation of ALMP, and the Chief Data Officer directorate, which has responsibility for data management, data integration, data access and security in alignment with ESDC's enterprise Data Strategy.

The evaluation directorate was able to build and grow its internal capacity on methodology and data by reducing its reliance on external experts and data collection efforts. By March 2022, the directorate allocated about ten people to this type of evaluation activity. This has allowed the directorate to become more ambitious in both scope and content of its work. For example, it has now started to conduct gender-based evaluations and is investing significant capacity into machine learning for the third cycle of evaluation, with the aim of even greater sub-group analysis of programme impacts.

By increasingly relying on administrative data and its internal capacity to conduct advanced quantitative analysis, the evaluation directorate has efficiently compartmentalised its resources to increase specialisation. It has three main areas of specialisation relating to its evaluation of LMDA across data preparation, impact analysis and organisation of analysis with PTs. The data preparation team ensures that data provided from CDO are assimilated and organised into the appropriate datasets for evaluation. The impact analysis team then works directly with these data, applying rigorous statistical techniques to estimate programme effects. A separate team manages interactions with PTs, including the organisation and planning of the joint evaluation work and the conduct of any qualitative research that is conducted locally.

The Chief Data Officer directorate was established in 2016, to oversee the department's data strategy. This has facilitated the establishment of data processes to embed best practices in data architecture and data management, processing, data development and data quality assurance. In line with its vision to drive towards better services and outcomes for clients by treating data as a shared, protected enterprise asset grounded in a culture of stewardship and collaboration, ESDC's strategy is guiding efforts to embed their data into a cloud infrastructure, streamlining data access protocols and ensuring a common standards for its different data products.

The separation of evaluation and policy within ESDC brings benefits and challenges. Centralising evaluation means that it is easier to co-ordinate evaluations, share expertise and gain through a coalescence of expertise in that area. The challenge is then to ensure priorities are aligned with policy and implementation work and that there is no duplication of work by analysts in other areas.

1.2.3. ESDC work with PTs to plan and implement evaluation

Extensive communication, organisation and collaboration are needed for ESDC and PTs to jointly plan and conduct the evaluation of the LMDA. Formal governance procedures and honest and accountable leadership have been cited as laying the foundations for this relationship between ESDC and PTs. Governance procedures mean that all parties have a voice in proceedings, formalised through an evaluation steering committee. The Forum of Labour Market Ministers, provides an avenue for ministers from federal, provincial and territorial levels to discuss higher-level issues. Its working groups allow for information sharing and discussion of issues between PTs and federal officials and ensure that any major issues arising from the evaluation work can be discussed further among senior policy makers.

1.3. Investments in data have been instrumental for conducting ALMP evaluation in Canada

1.3.1. Rich and accurate data are essential to conduct robust evaluations

Conducting evaluation of ALMPs requires the availability of high-quality data that are detailed enough to ensure that the estimates made are robust and reliable. Data are needed on what outcomes individuals enjoy subsequent to participation, including information on income and subsequent benefit receipt. Randomised studies, that ensure participants and non-participants are alike in every respect, require less data to estimate impact. Observational studies, where entry to the ALMPs is not controlled, have a higher data burden placed upon them, as these data are used to ensure that similar participants and non-participants are compared. Data can be collected in numerous ways. Administrative data are accurate, cheap, cover the full population but can be sparse in terms of, for example, the characteristics of programme participants beyond age and gender. Survey data offer greater opportunity to tailor data collection but come with added expense to collect, are difficult to collect in the same volume as administrative data and can suffer measurement issues. ESDC has made important improvements to its evaluation work by switching from survey-based data collection to using its administrative data linked to Canada Revenue Agency data on income.

1.3.2. Survey data were hugely expensive, slow to collect and prone to inaccuracy, issues that the use of linked administrative data came to resolve

In the first cycle of ALMP evaluation conducted by ESDC, data were collected via the use of surveys at the provincial level. This was primarily done to collect income data for participants, but given the observational nature of the evaluation, it was also necessary to gather detailed socio-economic data to compare alike participants and non-participants – on things like family status, education and previous employment. Samples also had to be drawn up from eligible non-participants to create a comparison group. This was both cumbersome and expensive. The surveys took a long time to plan and complete, entailing the use of external contractors to collect data. The resources required to conduct detailed surveys of individuals to any degree of scale entails a significant investment in personnel that government agencies rarely possess, instead contracting out to specialist external research firms is commonplace. Coupled with the existing analytical capacity within ESDC to manage these contractors at the time, this meant that a maximum of two to three studies could be ongoing at any point. This translated in the first cycle of evaluation taking around ten years to complete. The surveys were also prone to non-response, meaning oversampling was required to ensure sufficient sample size (increasing delivery cost). Recall error from survey participants also impacted the accuracy of the data collected.

Furthermore, once comprehensive comparisons were done between administrative data on earnings for participants and non-participants to the survey data collected from them, it revealed interesting recall errors, which were systematically related to participation. Participants in ALMPs were found to under-estimate their incomes, whilst non-participants were found to over-estimate their incomes. The systematic nature to these recall errors would cause programme impacts to be underestimated, leading to bias conclusions on their effectiveness. The move to administrative data improved accuracy as much as it reduced costs.

1.3.3. A linked data platform was created to enable efficient use of administrative data for evaluation

ESDC collated separate administrative data sources to establish the Labour Market Program Data Platform (LMPDP), a comprehensive platform for analysis, where data is anonymised to protect personal information. The LMPDP enables ESDC to look at a suite of information relating to ALMPs, including patterns of participation, eligibility for participation, patterns of employment insurance and social assistance receipt, annual sources of income, and annual job patterns. These data are compiled in different stages, taking the underlying data to create a unified dataset that is consistent and allow evaluation to be performed on it. Data are combined to ensure participation in various ALMPs is chronologically consistent. Patterns of eligibility for ALMPs are derived for non-participants, in order to construct a comparison group. Data from Canada Revenue Agency (CRA) are then added on to observe employment outcomes. The integration of the CRA data was vital in enabling ESDC to look at the impacts on employment income, one of the key requirements for any comprehensive ALMP assessment. These data also provided key information on social assistance receipt, which was not obtainable from a centralised register due to their delivery at the PT level. The creation of this platform ensures: efficient use of resource, so that data are not having to be continually re-worked; consistency across different evaluations; and institutional knowledge in the data is built up via their repeated use.

16 |

1.3.4. Rich information on past income and benefit receipt alongside socio-demographic data drive policy insights

ESDC integrates rich, but protected, information on individuals that is vital in conducting their counterfactual impact assessments. Socio-demographic and historic earnings and benefit data contained in the LMPDP provide a strong basis for which to compare alike individuals that did and did not participate in ALMPs. ESDC makes use of up to 75 socio-demographic and labour market variables, which are observed over five years prior to the participation period. Past patterns of income and benefit receipt are particularly important to serve as proxies for factors that are not captured in administrative data (for example, motivation or ability).

However, there are still some areas for which more data would be beneficial to inform the analysis. Data on education (e.g. field of study) would be particularly useful for young people, for whom there is limited information on their past income or benefit receipt to compare individuals with similar characteristics. Similarly having information on the presence of children would allow better consideration to be given on the labour market participation decisions of parents.

1.3.5. Data on outcomes allow a good assessment of ALMPs but could be extended to offer further insight

The use of linked administrative data means that outcomes analysis benefits from being accurate and comprehensive, permitting high-quality assessments to be made of how programmes influence participants' subsequent outcomes. A wide range of key aggregate outcomes are considered in the analysis. CRA data on employment income and on social assistance received in a year, are combined with ESDC employment insurance receipt data. This means that a full account can be given to the main sources of income that an individual might have in the period after participation.

However, due to data limitations, the current analysis does not consider issues of job quality, apart from earnings. Information on employment spells is not recorded in a central register and is not available via the CRA data, so analysis is unable to depict how ALMPs affect job tenure. Attachment to an employer, and whether participation has resulted in the individual finding a better match to job, which is reflected in part by employment duration, is not directly observed. Similarly, the type of contract that individuals are employed on, such as whether it is full-time or part-time, or on a permanent or temporary basis, is not observed in the administrative data. This type of information would help to build information on the impact of ALMPs on job dynamics.

Similarly, timeliness and aggregation of the data on income also impinge on the analysis. At present, income data are lagged two years behind the ALMP participation data and limit the ability for ESDC to produce up-to-date evaluation on their ALMPs. The annualised nature of the CRA income data also raises questions over their suitability to analyse the impact of job counselling programmes, whose benefits are comparatively short and smaller in scale. Assignment of earnings into post- and pre-programme years are non-trivial in such instances where the majority of the impact is likely to accrue in the same year as programme participation. Having more temporally disaggregated data would help to mitigate these issues.

1.4. ESDC evaluates operational programmes with robust techniques

ESDC use rigorous and credible methods to evaluate outcomes of their ALMPs. The ESDC evaluation strategy proceeds as an observational study. It does this because PTs already plan and deliver ALMPs to their citizens. ESDC then use data on this participation in ALMPs and attempt to compare similar participants and non-participants. This type of analysis is essential when policies are either already in operation, or it is not possible to test them prior to full scale roll-out. It means that it is not possible to control

ASSESSING CANADA'S SYSTEM OF IMPACT EVALUATION OF ACTIVE LABOUR MARKET POLICIES © OECD 2022 entry into programmes and efforts need to be made to find individuals that do not enrol on the programme but who are similar to those that do.

1.4.1. Observational techniques are combined to compare similar participant and non-participants

In order to conduct analysis in this manner, ESDC make use of their rich administrative data and employ methods that ensure that participants and non-participants are alike in every observable respect, apart from participation in the programme. The first stage of the analysis is to organise participant and non-participant groups so that the non-participants or participants that are not that similar to others are removed. This is done to reduce the computation and analytical processing time required in the subsequent stage. Participants and non-participants are then "matched" to each other, using the observable characteristics available in the administrative data. This aims to remove differences in outcomes between individuals that would have occurred even without programme participation. A final stage is then performed, so that only changes in outcomes between participants and non-participants are compared. Rather than compare income between participants and non-participants directly, the change in their income from the period before the programme to after the programme is compared. This helps to control for factors that may influence both programme participation and outcome variables but are not available in the administrative data. These methods are credible, respected and widespread in the academic literature. By comparing how the estimates change between the second and final stage of the analysis, ESDC can identify how sensitive the estimates are to the method used, lending greater ability for a discussion around how well the techniques used are able to control for differences between participants.

1.4.2. ESDC analyses packages of support and look at different groups of people according to their personal characteristics and past labour market experience

ESDC assesses packages of support, rather than individual programmes, which mean that these packages contain more than one individual programme. This is not a problem to the ESDC impact assessment itself, but it does make comparison across programmes slightly more difficult. By re-framing the analysis, so that it isolates the impact of a specific programme, it would facilitate comparisons between the different programmes offers.

Administrative data are used to split participants into different groups to analyse effects separately for different types of individuals. ESDC also uses the administrative data to look at other groups of interest, including youth, older workers, long-tenured workers, gender, ethnicity, immigration, and self-identification of being a "visible minority" or having a disability. This then allows ESDC to evaluate whether programmes are more or less effective for different groups of individuals.

The third cycle of evaluation will see ESDC explore the use of machine learning algorithms to look at effect "heterogeneity" – a systematic data-driven way to reveal differences in programme outcomes for individuals (rather than on aggregate) that does not rely on a pre-specified disaggregation by the researcher. Machine learning algorithms also have the potential to automate parts of the process of analysis and remove the need for as much user-expertise in compiling estimators. This will offer an interesting opportunity to test whether significant further variation of participants is found by disaggregating them further.

1.4.3. Individuals not currently claiming employment insurance are analysed separately

In addition to the sub-group analysis looking at different personal characteristics, ESDC separates out completely those ALMP participants without a current employment insurance claim. This is done primarily due to the problem of constructing a reliable counterfactual group of non-participants for these former employment insurance claimants using the administrative data. There are concerns that motivation for this group, which is unobservable in the administrative data, might be an influencing factor in participation in ALMPs. This would potentially mean estimates of ALMPs would be biased upwards (if motivation increased participation likelihood and also earnings). ESDC employs a clever technique to address some of the concerns for this group by re-basing the comparison group to be those former employment insurance claimants who participate in job counselling only, the least intensive ALMP offered. By doing this, ESDC is able to compare participants in other programmes to this group, but is able to resolve concerns around motivation for participation, by comparing with individuals who have already volunteered for the other programme. This comes with the expense of not being able to estimate the effect that job counselling itself has on these individuals.

1.4.4. Sensitivity analysis is conducted to evaluate uncertainty and corroborate results

ESDC conducts checks across a wide range of different areas of the analysis to ensure that results are as reliable and credible as possible. Tests are done to ensure estimates are not sensitive to the inclusion or omission of variables. Large changes in estimates if this were the case would suggest the estimates did not give a good general assessment of the programme's impact on participants. ESDC uses statistical tests to aid selection of the variables it includes in its statistical analysis, reducing the room for human error. Tests are also conducted to ensure that all participants and non-participants selected have an individual that is sufficiently alike to them. There are several different algorithms that can be used to compare individuals to one another and ESDC utilises a range of these algorithms to demonstrate that their central use of algorithm is not significantly different from the others available, lending weight to the stability of the estimates. It also inspects whether differences in outcome variables between participants and non-participants are stable in the pre-programme participation period. This is crucial to the final step of their analysis, where pre- and post-programme outcome differences are compared.

Comparing the results from the regional analysis for PTs to the overall results for Canada, could provide more insight into whether the estimates give a good general assessment of a specific programme. Splitting the whole original dataset randomly into two and using the first half to estimate the statistical parameters before applying these to the second half, would also permit further insight on the ability of the estimates to give a good general assessment of the ALMPs.

1.5. Quality assurance processes are conducted using internal and external resource

Quality assurance is rigorous and high quality external peer reviewers are used to guide analysis. ESDC has implemented a set of corporate procedures on quality assurance to conduct analysis and ensure that methods and outputs are shared with expert external peer reviewers for feedback.

1.5.1. In-house quality assurance procedures and accumulated institutional knowledge ensure analysis is conducted thoroughly, minimising errors

The establishment of an in-house methodology unit has allowed ESDC to develop guidelines on the processes to follow in evaluations. Separating out this process from the team conducting the evaluation allows specialisation – guidance is developed independently and so the risk that the extent and nature of the checks in place is being driven by the analysis that has been conducted is reduced. Guidelines and processes are developed from first principles. Each of the stages developed has multiple checks to complete to ensure data accuracy and methodological rigour, comprising checks on data use, checks on the code to extract data and run analysis, reviews of methodological development for rigour and checks on analytical outputs for consistency.

Also important has been the continued tenure of many of the analytical team, a core of whom have been in post since the beginning, or close to the beginning of the shift towards in-house delivery. This has meant that expertise has been built around them that is cognisant of the gaps, knows the organisational and policy boundaries and is able to plan for change. Staff retention in this respect cannot be underestimated. Investments have been made so that data and methodology are properly documented, to lay the foundations for future analysts and as this will be critical to ensure business continuity with the passage of time as gradually a new generation of ESDC officials take the helm.

EDSC analytical staff have also presented their work to numerous academic and government conference audiences to benefit further from socialisation of techniques and results and the discussion that ensues from this.

1.5.2. External peer reviewers provide expertise on methodology and outputs

Throughout the period of development of in-house expertise, constant engagement with peer reviewers has provided a critical sounding board to develop methodological strategies and ensure ongoing professional development for ESDC analysts, learning practically from experts in the field whilst conducting their work. A feature of this work has been the sustained use of the same peer reviewers providing both continuity and enabling the reviewers to build a deep understanding of the policy landscape and data availability. It also facilitated a deeper understanding of the skillset of the ESDC analytical team for the peer reviewers, so that insights are both rich and nuanced, fully exploiting the abilities of both the reviewers and the in-house team.

The use of peer reviewers has allowed ESDC to conduct analysis in-house whilst maintaining the ability to conduct credible analysis using the most up-to-date techniques. When countries decide on whether to contract-out analysis or to conduct it internally, quality assurance is a key consideration. By contracting-out, it is possible to choose institutions with the specialised expertise necessary to conduct evaluations. If this work is carried-out internally, resources need to be employed directly. ESDC has employed a hybrid model, whereby analysts are employed within ESDC to carry out the technical analytical work, but academic peer reviewers are employed to advise on both techniques, data queries and on reviewing the outputs from the work, including initial advice on the data and underlying quantitative data methodology to utilise. This has allowed ESDC to develop institutional knowledge and expertise on the methods used as the evaluations have progressed.

1.6. ESDC conducts full cost-benefit analysis of ALMPs

ESDC take their impact assessments a step further to consider the value for money offered by ALMPs. Often evaluation studies stop short of a full assessment of the worth of a programme by only considering outcomes for the participants. A participant may earn CAD 1 000 more following an intervention, but if it cost CAD 2000 to deliver the programme, it may not make sense to proceed with it. Only looking at the change in earnings precludes the ability to make these assessments. ESDC conducts a full cost-benefit analysis of its ALMPs, with several years of post-programme follow-up. This assessment is only possible because ESDC has already used robust techniques to isolate the impacts on earnings and benefit receipt that are solely attributable to the programme. Not only does this allow federal government and PTs to make planning decisions secure in the knowledge of the return on their investment but by evaluating programmes individually, it allows PTs to make assessments as to the relative mix of programmes they choose to allocate funding. Alongside producing a central cost-benefit estimate, it also varies the assumptions it uses for three key variables: how values in future years are adjusted to provide a present value; changes in the cost to society of using government funds for programming; and changes in the time horizon over which costs and benefits are accrued. This demonstrates how sensitive the results are to these variables. ESDC also details wider costs and benefits that it does not account for in the analysis including benefits to mental and physical well-being, effects on crime, and spillovers to the broader economy.

Extending this cost benefit analysis by including a number of additions to the analysis, would give ESDC the ability to make an even more powerful and comprehensive assessment of its ALMPs. Because of the re-distributive nature of ALMPs, which help those relatively more disadvantaged individuals, sensitivity analysis to weight the outcomes of the policy (by estimating the difference in income between those participating in the ALMPs and the average income of taxpayers and using this to calculate the extra benefit these individuals receive as a result of the income transfer to them) can help to ensure that the benefits of participation are fully accounted for. The value of an additional dollar of income for someone further down the income scale is potentially higher than for someone with a higher income. Providing additional sensitivity analysis that demonstrates how much difference this makes to estimates, ESDC would be better able to position the benefits of its ALMPs relative to other policies which are less redistributive in nature. Full incorporation of data on health outcomes would allow a more holistic view of the potential benefits of work on individuals' underlying health and the subsequent impact on people themselves and on government outlays. In addition, extensions to existing work looking at the uncertainty around cost-benefit estimates would allow a more refined communication of the plausible range of outcomes.

1.7. Canada could enlarge the research base by making data available to external researchers

At present the analysis on ALMPs can only be conducted by the evaluation directorate within ESDC due to privacy and protection of personal information requirements. Whilst resources have been increased over the years to permit more in-house evaluation work, the extent of the analysis conducted is constrained by the limitations of this resource. Increasing data availability to external researchers, would facilitate evaluation of ALMPs, promoting innovation and providing useful cross-reference for the existing work done by ESDC.

Statistics Canada is leading the way in increasing data availability to researchers, offering two different access routes – unrestricted access to carefully de-identified data, or restricted access, which is facilitated at Research Data Centres and offers the possibility of access to a wider range of data. However, even with the unrestricted access it is currently impossible to conduct evaluation of ALMPs, because it does not house data needed on ALMP participation. However, data is held on CRA income and employment insurance receipt, so most of the underlying data used by ESDC is available, meaning that the sole addition of ALMP participation data (already used by ESDC in their evaluations) would permit the conduct of ALMP evaluation.

Many countries have made these data available to researchers and benefit from the expansion of resources this engenders. Some facilitate this using quasi-governmental research bodies (such as the *Institut für Arbeitsmarkt* in Germany or the Institute for Labour Market Policy Evaluation in Sweden). These bodies help both to share data but also to focus the resources needed to conduct the research within the same institution. Others organise access like Canada, through statistics institutions. Statistics Finland offers a good example of the range of data that might be organised and shared via these institutions. Making small expansions to the data available through Statistics Canada, which builds on the joint evaluation work already conducted by PTs and ESDC, by sharing PTs data on ALMP participation, would make great strides in democratising data access and the ability to open up evaluation to external researchers.

1.8. ESDC could benefit from randomised studies which can help to systematically build knowledge

One area which merits further consideration by ESDC is the use of randomised studies to evaluate different aspects of policy delivery. By keeping trials small it would allow policy questions to be evaluated without significantly impacting upon existing delivery. It also allows trials to be managed more easily. As expertise was built, or demand for them increased, they could be scaled up accordingly.

As PTs have significant flexibility in their delivery of ALMPs, it means there is a wide variation in how programmes are delivered, for example, whether they are delivered in-house by provincial government or out-sourced to external contractors. Similarly the precise content of the programmes can vary, for example around the intensity of the job counselling services offered. These issues have not currently been addressed in the evaluation work that has taken place, which concentrates more on the aggregate value-for-money of programmes (what the value for money of training is against no training, rather than say looking at the intensity of training).

Trials are useful because they allow a careful exploration of such policy questions and can be designed to produce evidence on specific policy designs of interest. Randomisation also allows for more robust estimates as it ensures that only effects attributable to the programme are produced. Denmark offers an example where a co-ordinated approach to randomised studies over time has allowed them to systematically address evidence gaps on their policies. By giving thought to precisely how PTs deliver policy, questions on the best structure and delivery mode for ALMPs can be addressed by ESDC and allow policy to be improved beyond broader comparisons of overall programme type (for example, is a more intensive training programme better, rather than just comparing training to counselling services). Trials can also complement the existing evaluation work conducted by ESDC, as they allow both to be done simultaneously. A small trial does not disrupt the ongoing delivery of ALMPs to individuals and can allow innovation to occur without a significant change to delivery in the meantime. Canada has implemented a Future Skills strategy that includes its Future Skills Centre, which already offers the opportunity to independently run such trials on ALMPs that aim to build skills.

ESDC has constantly innovated its evaluation strategy and is now moving towards the vanguard of policy evaluation techniques. Much of this is done iteratively. ESDC and PTs use their evaluation committee to review progress and establish priorities and work streams. Conducting analysis in cycles provides a natural breakpoint for review.

1.9. ESDC makes good efforts to communicate the results of its ALMP evaluations but more could be done to reach a broader audience

The conduct of evaluation work in ESDC proceeds in an open and transparent fashion. Evaluation reports are published for Canada and all of the participating PTs separately, detailing the impact assessments made for each of the underlying ALMPs. This allows ESDC to tell a positive story about its ALMPs, using the evidence generated on their value for money. The requirement in bi-lateral agreements to cyclically evaluate ALMPs has provided a useful checkpoint that ensures evaluation is carried out routinely, meaning that it cannot succumb to budgetary or political pressures.

The combination of a federal evaluation framework and work within ESDC to foster transparency, means that ALMP evaluation work programmes are well defined, clear and accountable. The federal Policy on Results, which was introduced in 2016, sets out clear obligations for ministries on evaluation conduct and publication. Furthermore, the ESDC evaluation directorate published a paper in 2017 in the Canadian Journal of Program Evaluation that set out the motives and rationale behind the evaluation strategy. In addition, its effort to present its work at external seminars, serve not only as usual peer review but as a means by which to foster this transparency. Jointly, these efforts means that a clear and coherent ALMP evaluation work programme is visible and transparent to the public.

However, adjustments could be made to further improve the reach and understanding of ESDC communication. More could be done to tailor communication to different audiences and ensure that messages are shared in the right format and forums. The Jobeffekter website, of the Danish Agency for Labour Market and Recruitment, offers a good example of how evaluation information can be packaged into different bundles, so that readers of different technical ability can find information that is accessible to them. Jargon could be better avoided and messages focussed so that they are more easily understood and meaningful in communications. Better promotion of analytical work, via social media and news channels, would mean that analysis could reach further. In the United States, MDRC uses newsletters and social media channels to share its work with wider audiences, encouraging greater dissemination. Publication of the peer review summaries, which are collected by ESDC in the course of the evaluation of ALMPs, would help to further promote trust and understanding of the evaluation.

Key policy recommendations

Continue to invest in linked administrative data to refine analysis

- Work directly, or via Statistics Canada, with the provinces and territories (PTs) to gather administrative data on educational attainment. These data are particularly important when trying to make inferences on young people, who do not have a long history of labour market participation, to proxy skills, competence and motivation.

- Consider incorporation of wider data on adult skills to see whether programmes encourage individuals to gain further skills. Particularly, for programmes such as Job Creation Partnerships, whose initial aim may be to move individuals closer to the labour market rather than to a job immediately.

- Invest efforts to obtain more detailed information on childcare, particularly on the age of children. Labour market participation decisions, particularly so for women, are often motivated by events correlated with the ages of children, e.g. birth, attending school and leaving home. Without these data, it makes valid inference for these individuals problematic. Similarly acquiring data on immigrants (country of birth, time of arrival in Canada) would allow policy makers to evaluate how ALMPs help this specific group of individuals.

- Lobby for access to high quality real-time income and tax information, to substantially speed up analysis, which are currently delayed by two years after the ALMP participation data.

- Explore what further data could be added to facilitate assess job quality outcomes, including transitions into and out of work and information on contract type. Changes to existing Record of Employment data may provide an avenue for incorporation in existing data gathering. This would also require improvements to coverage of these data.

Continue process to open up data access to external researchers to leverage a wider pool of analysis and expertise

- Make ALMP participation data available through Statistics Canada to benefit from research that external academics and research institutions can provide in generating knowledge, cross-validating ESDC research and providing innovation. This has the benefit of providing additional insights into policy and offering the analysis teams within ESDC further ideas for future data exploration.

- Routinely opening access to CRA datasets to PTs via Statistics Canada would make it much easier for PTs to conduct their own analyses of the ALMPs that they deliver. Presently many have no access to this data, or go through laborious routes for access, which limits their ability to actively scrutinise their own policy analysis (or to liaise with researchers to conduct the analysis if they do not have their own analytical capacity).

Consider trials at PTs level to provide greater insight

- Currently, federal analysis looks at rather aggregate issues of whether a programme bring gains relative to not having the programme. This overlooks the variation in delivery modes and service offerings within PTs.
- A systematic programme of small-scale trials would allow ESDC to more easily ask questions about service design and delivery that it is not possible to answer with the current evaluation toolkit. It would allow ESDC to further evaluate value for money in order to promote the efficient use of public funds, rather than simply asking whether or not a programme should exist in its entirety.
- A randomised trial would also mean the issue of finding a suitable comparison group for former employment insurance claimants is removed and comparisons could be made on a like-for-like basis across current employment insurance claimants in terms of programme impacts.

Consider small additions to the cost-benefit analysis to improve coverage and robustness

- Incorporate information on health to reflect the impact of outcomes in the labour market on broader individual health.
- Include variations in the main outcome variables (income, employment insurance, social assistance) in sensitivity analysis. Consider using Monte-Carlo analysis to build a richer understanding of the likely range of outputs.
- Additional sensitivity analysis to weight cost-benefit outcomes for participants to reflect the relative impact of ALMPs on individuals at the lower end of the income distribution. The marginal impact of an extra dollar of income is greater for those with lower incomes than it is for those with high incomes. As ESDC analysis shows, this is true of ALMP delivery. Therefore consideration should be given as to whether a distributional weighting to reflect these factors would help to better contextualise ESDC impact assessment relative to those from other Ministries where this may be less likely to be the case.

Publish summaries of peer reviewers to build upon the existing framework of openness and transparency

- Publishing summaries of academic peer reviewers on the ESDC website would increase transparency and public trust in the results of the evaluations by ESDC.

Separate analysis to allow greater insight on methodological assumptions

- ESDC conducts two stages in its impact assessment. A more detailed discussion, comparing the results of each stage, would allow ESDC to show how much the estimates change and demonstrate the sensitivity of the analysis to the assumptions made.
- Consider reporting on programmes individually, rather than as combinations, to facilitate comparison across programmes.
- Split original data randomly into two to estimate the statistical model on one half and test its ability to match participants and non-participants in the second half. This would help to determine whether the model provides an overview of participants that generalises well.

Review outputs to ensure accessibility and maximise delivery of key messages

- Avoid the use of jargon in non-technical summaries.
- Make sure key results are included in all briefing material and stand-out from the rest of the information.
- Pro-actively share research results using social media and online channels

Re-establish opportunities for in-person information sharing among PTs

- Communication and collaboration are vital elements in making regional delivery of policy work effectively. One aspect of this, viewed positively by PTs, is the opportunity to come together and discuss their respective operational and delivery perspectives. These face-to-face opportunities were suspended because of the COVID-19 pandemic. Efforts should be re-made to renew these opportunities as soon as permitted by sanitary conditions.

Note

[1] These cycles refer to the evaluation of the Labour Market Development Agreements, the main federal funding vehicle for ALMP.

2 Delivery and analysis of active labour market policies in Canada

Employment and Social Development Canada (ESDC), the federal ministry with responsibility for employment insurance and active labour market policy (ALMP), is responsible for policy decisions and provides funding to provinces and territories (PTs) who are required under the labour market transfers, to consult annually with labour market stakeholders in their respective jurisdictions to inform the appropriate mix of programmes to support their local populations. The Labour Market Development Agreements (LMDA) is the largest ALMP package in Canada. It provides employment support services and training, which together accounted for around CAD 2 billion of the total 2019 spending of CAD 5 billion on ALMPs. A highly capable analytical team within ESDC has conducted impact assessment of the LMDA since 2010, demonstrating that ALMPs offer value-for-money to the taxpayer. Analysts have worked closely with policy colleagues and officials from the PTs to ensure evaluation plans are agreed collaboratively.

2.1. Introduction

In 2019, prior to the pandemic, Canada's federal government invested around CAD 5 billion in active labour market policies (ALMPs) to help individuals find work. Employment and Social Development Canada (ESDC) is the government ministry with federal responsibility to improve the standard of living and quality of life for its citizens via the promotion of a highly skilled labour force and an efficient and inclusive labour market. Given its mandate, ESDC provides a portfolio of programmes aim to improve skills development in Canada. The largest programmes take the form of transfer payments to provinces and territories via the Labour Market Transfer Agreements (LMTAs), which encompass two distinct funding streams:

- The **Labour Market Development Agreements** (LMDAs) provide eligible individuals with programmes such as skills training, recruitment and start-up subsidies, direct job creation and employment support services (including employment assistance services providing lighter touch interventions such as employment counselling, job search assistance and needs assessments). Eligible participants must be actively claiming employment insurance, have previously completed an employment insurance claim in the last five years, or have minimum employment insurance premium contributions in at least five of the previous ten years. Employment assistance services are open to all Canadians, regardless of previous work and contribution histories.

- The **Workforce Development Agreements** (WDAs) fund training and employment support for individuals and employers regardless of their employment status, including those that have no ties to the employment insurance. The WDAs support individuals with weaker labour force attachment and include specific funding targeted for persons with disabilities. They are also used to support members of underrepresented groups (such as Indigenous peoples, youth, older workers, and newcomers to Canada). The agreements also allow provision of supports to employers seeking to train current or new employees.

In 2019, Canada transferred CAD 2.35 billion in funding to PTs via the LMDAs, covering 630 000 clients and 970 000 interventions (ESDC, 2021[1]). Its WDAs provide for annual funding for CAD 720 million, and a further annual top-up of CAD 150 million (CAD 900 million spread over six years from 2017/18 to 2022/23). Due to the nature of this funding and the flexibility in its delivery, ESDC do not collate participant data in the same manner as the LMDAs. Some other smaller funding streams also exist to deliver ALMPs. Most notably the federal Indigenous Skills and Employment Training Program provides annual funding of CAD 410 million from 2019 to 2028 (ESDC, 2020[2]) for ALMPs that are similar in type to the LMDAs, but targeted at the Indigenous Canadian population.

While the Government of Canada provides funding and sets parameters under the LMDAs and the WDAs, provinces and territories consult with labour market stakeholders in their jurisdictions to set priorities and inform the design and delivery of employment programs and services that meet the needs of their local labour markets. This is subject to the constraints laid down in the legislation and/or in the agreements for the different funding streams. For the LMDAs, this is the 1996 Employment Insurance Act, which governs the types of programmes and services that PTs may offer. Policy makers in ESDC are interested in which of these programmes work and for whom, so that future policy changes are cognisant of the available evidence and deliver the best outcomes for Canadians.

Skills training in Canada is a shared responsibility between the federal government and PTs. At the federal level, programming focuses on issues of national and strategic importance, that extend beyond local and regional labour markets. For example, programming to advance research and innovation, to support those further from the labour market and to engage employers in demand-driven training is considered at the federal level. Since devolution of federal training programmes to PTs in the mid-1990s, PTs have developed expertise in programme design, built up training infrastructure, and established relationships with stakeholders to deliver training aligned with their specific labour market conditions. In addition to programming offered under the LMDAs and WDAs, PTs deliver programming funded from their own revenues.

This report focusses on information from the quantitative evaluation of the LMDAs. There are a few principle reasons for this. The first is that it represents the largest and most significant body of work that ESDC undertake with respect to impact evaluation of ALMPs and the LMDAs are the primary funding stream for delivery of ALMPs. The second is that the underlying dataset created for evaluation of the LMDAs – the Labour Market Program Data Platform (see Annex B of ESDC (2020[3])) – and the techniques employed in the LDMA evaluation have been subsequently adopted for use in evaluation of other, smaller funding streams (Indigenous Skills and Employment Training (ESDC, 2020[2]), and the Youth Employment and Skills Strategy (ESDC, 2020[4]; 2020[3])).[1] The most significant omission is the lack of evaluation of the WDAs. The WDAs were first implemented in 2017-18, so it has not yet been possible to complete evaluation on them. However, findings from the third cycle of LMDA evaluation, may help inform the effectiveness of certain type of WDAs interventions for some participant sub-groups. Separate WDA evaluation is also being conducted. Understanding the effects of the WDAs programming will be important to ensure that funding decisions can be made on the overall package of support to jobseekers that is able to contextualise the pros and cons of the different elements alongside each other.

2.2. Active labour market policy spending

2.2.1. Canada spends less than the OECD average supporting jobseekers

Canada is below the OECD average on both passive and active labour market spending. In 2019 it spent around 0.5% GDP on passive measures and 0.2% of GDP on active measures (Figure 2.1). In terms of spending per unemployed person on active measures, this placed it 23rd out of the 32 OECD countries for which there are data, a fall from its rank of 18th in 2004. In this context, it is apparent that ensuring the money available is spent on programmes that ensure the best outcomes for individuals is vitally important. Because the amount of federal funding for the LMDAs has been fixed in nominal terms since its inception, it may explain in part why Canada's ranking has declined relative to other OECD countries. Explicit top-ups of funding have to occur in order to increase spending, which mean spending does not automatically adjust to changes in demand.

Figure 2.1. Canada spends 20% less than the OECD average on passive measure and 50% less on active measures

Spending on active and passive labour market measures as a share of GDP

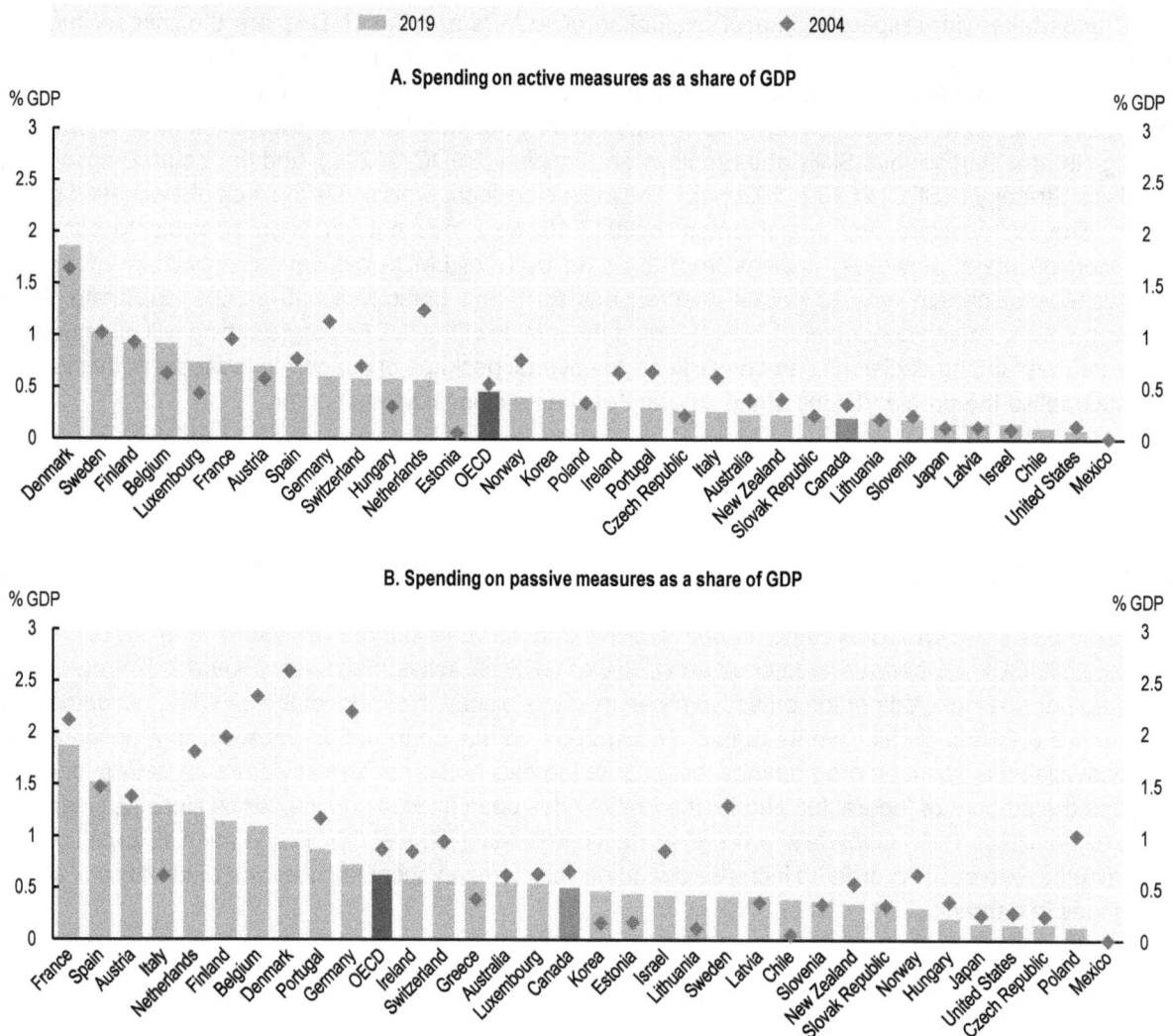

Note: OECD is an unweighted average. 2019 data for Australia and New Zealand for employment incentives and for passive measures refers to budget year July 2018 to June 2019 and not July 2019 to June 2020 unlike for the other ALMPs as this category was highly affected by the exceptional measures taken to address the challenges of COVID-19. Similarly data for passive measures for the United States refers to 2018.
Source: *OECD Database on Public expenditure and participant stocks on LMP*, http://stats.oecd.org//Index.aspx?QueryId=8540.

StatLink https://stat.link/nvdo3t

These dynamics can be seen clearly when real spending on active measures per unemployed jobseeker over time is analysed (in terms of 2020 price levels). From the mid-1990s Canada spent around CAD 5 000 per unemployed jobseeker on active measures. Following the 2008 Financial Crisis this reduced to around CAD 4 000 and has never really recovered. In the decade to 2019, spending was some 22% lower per person than the decade to 2008 (Figure 2.2).

Figure 2.2. ALMP spending per unemployed person in Canada has fallen in the decade to 2019

Real spending per unemployed person (15-64) on active labour market programmes (ALMPs)

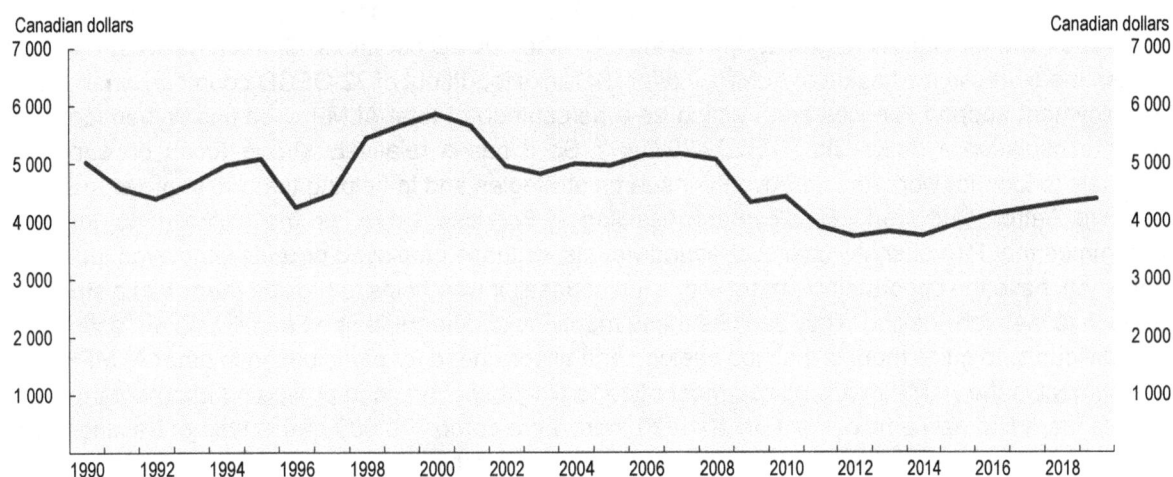

Note: Spending deflating using the consumer price index (CPI) taking 2020 as the base year.
Source: OECD Databases: *Public expenditure and participant stocks on LMP*, http://stats.oecd.org//Index.aspx?QueryId=8540 for spending, *Main Economic Indicators Publication* http://stats.oecd.org//Index.aspx?QueryId=17074 for CPI and *LFS by Sex and Age* http://dotstat.oecd.org//Index.aspx?QueryId=9571 for unemployed persons.

StatLink 🔗 https://stat.link/jv7lpi

2.2.2. A range of ALMPs are offered to Canada's citizens via the LMDAs

The LMDAs are designed to help eligible clients into employment and to secure better jobs. To do this, they comprise a combination of different programmes to meet different needs. Table 2.1 maps the different programmes according to the type of service. The only notable omission from the main ALMP categories is category five, supported employment and rehabilitation. Programmes in this category are provided under a separate set of funding in the Opportunities Fund for Persons with Disabilities.

Table 2.1. LMDA offer a basket of different ALMPs

LMDA Name	ALMP Categorisation	Description
Targeted Wage Subsidy (TWS)	Employment Incentives (Category 4)	Encourage employers to hire individuals who they would not normally hire in the absence of a subsidy
Self-Employment Assistance (SE)	Start-up Incentives (Category 7)	Help individuals to create jobs for themselves by starting a business
Job Creation Partnerships (JCP)	Direct Job Creation (Category 6)	Provide individuals with opportunities through which they can gain work experience that leads to on-going employment
Skills Development (SD)	Training (Category 2)	Help individuals obtain skills, ranging from basic to advanced skills through direct assistance to individuals
Employment Assistance Services (EAS)	Placement and Related Services (Category 1)	Provide employment services such as counselling, developing a career or training plan, and job search assistance

Note: Classification according to the OECD LMP database, please see https://www.oecd.org/els/emp/Coverage-and-classification-of-OECD-data-2015.pdf.

2.2.3. Employment Assistance Services and Skills Development comprise the majority of the ALMPs offered

In the five years to 2019/20, Employment Assistance Services and Skills Development accounted for 88% of total spending on LMDAs (Figure 2.3).[2] Relative to other OECD countries, Canada has a strong focus on these measures in the basket of ALMPs it offers. It ranks fourth out of 32 OECD countries when looking at employment support services and training as a percentage of total ALMP spending. When looking at training in isolation it ranks fifth (OECD, 2021[5]).[3] So it has a relatively strong focus on supporting individuals to look for work and improve their search strategies and in helping them to improve their skills to secure better paid work. Employment Assistance Services serve as the gateway to the extra programmes that PTs offer. All unemployed individuals, or those employed or underemployed looking for a better job, have the opportunity to meet with a job counsellor who helps to provide them with a structured approach to their job seeking. They can use these meetings to determine need and create an "action plan" with individuals, to guide them in their job seeking and assess need for participation in other ALMPs. Skills Development is the ALMP that it utilised most often to aid jobseekers to improve and augment their skills and help them find new employment. In 2019/20 there were some 170 000 of this type of training-related interventions compared to 25 000 of the other programmes combined.

In the share of the LMDAs programme spending, removing Employment Assistance Services due to their universal nature, Targeted Wage Subsidies have seen the largest growth from 9% in 2014/15 to 13.4% in 2019/20. Job Creation Partnerships share has grown by 24% and represented some 3.6% of spending by 2019/20. Both Skills Development and Self-Employment have seen reductions in their share of spending. While Skills Development still receives the lion's share of the combined programme spending, this relative shift towards the other programmes is at least consistent with the evidence from Canada that in value for money terms they offer particularly good returns to society (ESDC, 2017[6]).

Figure 2.3. Employment Assistance Services and Skills Development comprise the majority of the spending

Spending on individuals programmes in the labour market development agreements (LMDA) by year

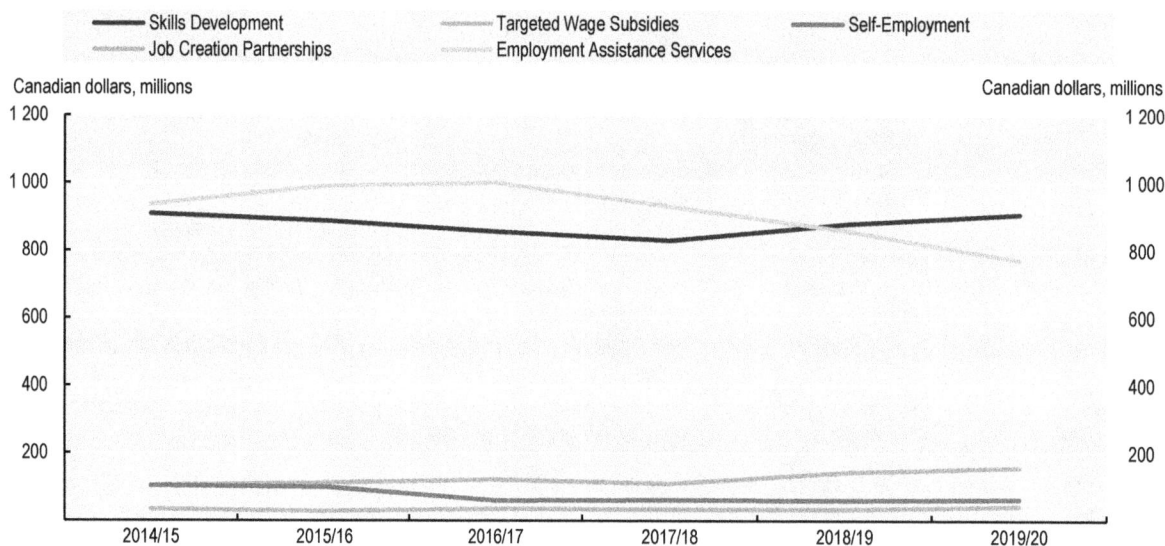

Note: Author's aggregation of administrative information from annual employment insurance Monitoring and Assessment reports.
Source: Employment and Social Development Canada, (ESDC), employment insurance Monitoring and Assessment Report, (2016-2021).

StatLink 🔗 https://stat.link/syltiq

2.3. ALMP effectiveness

To scrutinise the effectiveness of the ALMPs that ESDC offers, it conducts extensive evaluation of the LMDAs and their underlying ALMPs. This incorporates a range of outcome indicators to inform their impact on labour market attachment. These indicators include the likelihood of employment, earnings in employment and subsequent receipt of employment insurance and social assistance. Comparing the combination of these indicators for participants and non-participants with similar characteristics, alongside data on costs of delivering the programmes, allows ESDC to determine how much value for money ALMPs provide.

2.3.1. ALMPs are effective, but with some variation between and within programmes

The impact assessments conducted by ESDC demonstrate that programmes are effective in helping individuals to advance in the labour market (ESDC, 2017[6]). However there is variation in the effectiveness between programmes (for example, Skills Development has a larger average employment effect than Employment Assistance Services) and variation within the same programme across different regions (for example, Skills Development employment effects vary from 2 percentage points to 10 percentage points across PTs).

Figure 2.4 shows that effects on the incidence of employment, differences between PTs for the same programme are larger than the average national differences across programmes. Similar patterns hold for the other outcome variables evaluated.

Figure 2.4. There is greater variation between regions in the same programme than there is across programme types

Impact on incidence of employment by programme type and region, active claimants

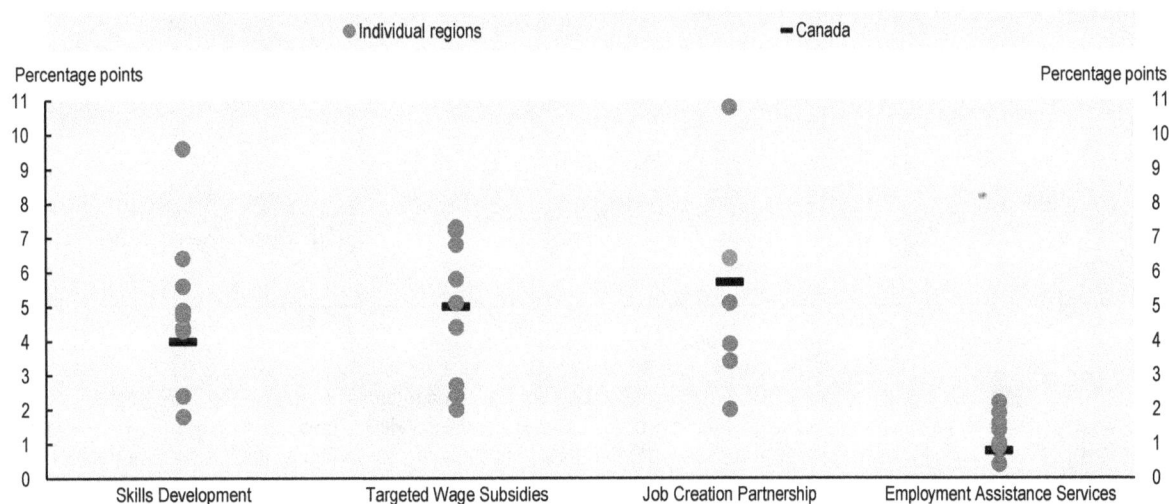

Note: Results for provinces and territories (PTs) are contained separately in the individual reports. They have been compiled here and each individual PTs estimate is a separate data point. The series for Canada has been extracted from the aggregate evaluation report on Canada.
Source: Individual Employment and Social Development Canada (ESDC) impact assessment reports on provinces and territories (2017-2018), available at www.canada.ca.

StatLink ⫘ https://stat.link/pzqj40

Variation is also evident when looking into heterogeneous effects across groups of individuals. In fact, there is a greater variation when looking at different groups of people, than there is when looking at different regions (Figure 2.5). There could be numerous reasons to expect different programme impacts for different group of individuals, dependent on their underlying challenge in the labour market. For instance, if older workers were discriminated against in the labour market, then a skills development intervention, that demonstrated their proficiency in a particular subject, might unlock more job activities for them relative to the average participant, if it removed that discrimination in addition to adding skills. Without specific and detailed evaluation of the underlying causal mechanisms of these effects on sub-groups though, it is impossible to be precise on the reason why differences occur.

Presently, the analysis conducted by ESDC (2017[6]) cannot distinguish to what extent these differences in outcomes between regions are driven by policy implementation differences, differences in the eligible population or regional labour markets differences. This could be addressed by looking at whether treatment effects differ by PTs in the aggregate assessment for Canada, or by weighting the individual PTs outcomes into a Canadian average of jobseeker groups. Doing this would provide further insights on the extent to which policy delivery choices drive outcomes and could lead to the development of an analytical programme of work designed to provide further evidence on this.

Figure 2.5. There is a greater variation in outcomes for different groups of people than there is for different regions

Skills Development, impact on incidence of employment, active claimants

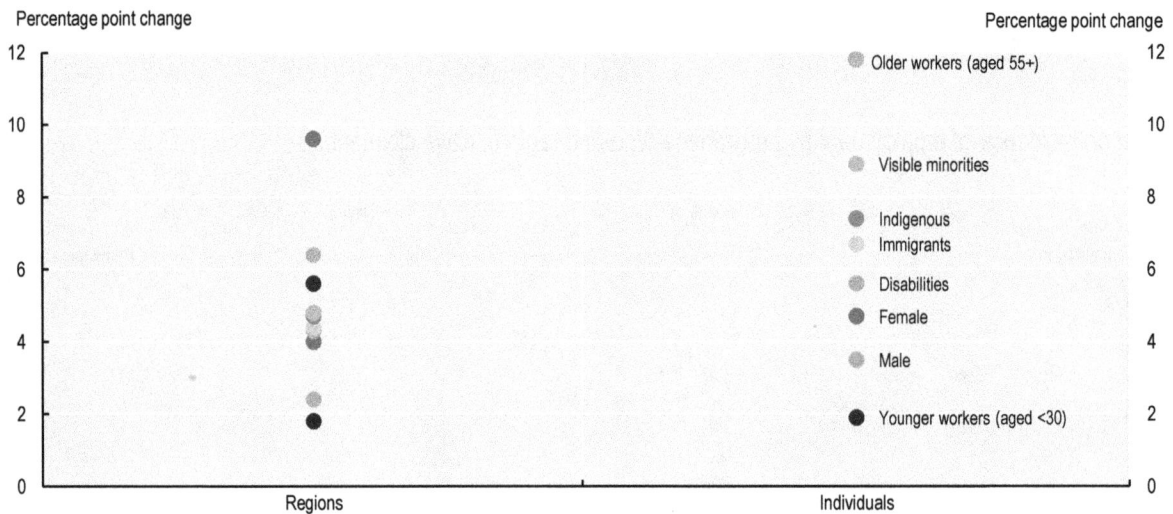

Note: Regions taken from Cycle II labour market development agreement (LMDA) analysis, for individual cohorts 2002-05. Individuals taken from Cycle III analysis for individual cohorts 2010-12. Aggregate impacts for Canada are the same across these two reports, though the breakdowns reported here may not be. Neither report series has both breakdowns contained within. The comparison between them is made for illustration only. "Visible minority" refers to whether a person identifies as a visible minority, as defined by the Employment Equity Act. The Employment Equity Act defines visible minorities as "persons, other than Aboriginal peoples, who are non-Caucasian in race or non-white in colour". "Indigenous" indicates whether the client identifies themselves as of Aboriginal origin. "Disability" refers to individuals with a self-identified disability.
Source: Individual Employment and Social Development Canada (ESDC) impact assessment reports on provinces and territories (2017-2018) available at www.canada.ca for regions and ESDC (2021), *Analysis of Employment Benefits and Support Measures (EBSM) Profile and Medium-Term Incremental Impacts* from 2010 to 2017 (unpublished), for individuals.

StatLink 🔗 https://stat.link/bheotk

Knowing to what extent differences between regions are driven by compositional differences in the eligible jobseekers is important in the Canadian context, given the considerable flexibility afforded to the PTs to design and deliver programme supports and services. Differences in policy design and implementation across PTs may play a role in how effective programmes are at securing better work for individuals. These issues are pertinent in most OECD countries, as even in situations where policies are designed nationally, there is room for significant variation in how they are implemented in different localities, even when centrally by one central agency.

Differences in the delivery costs of PTs are large (Figure 2.6). Aside from broad legislative definitions of programme types, PTs have the flexibility to choose the precise nature and content of these programmes. In addition, programmes may be delivered centrally by regional administrations, or contracted out and delivered by third party partners. Therefore, the potential for significant differences in programme delivery between PTs is large.

Skills Development has the smallest proportional difference between the lowest and highest PTs average cost- even here, it costs 2.3 times as much to deliver the programme in the PT with the highest average cost compares to the PT with the lowest average. The important point is not the comparison of costs per se – a higher delivery cost may be more than justified if the outcomes are better, or if redistribution is a particular concern. But without knowing how the composition of programme delivery affects outcomes, it is difficult to give any particular insight into how programmes should be designed to provide better outcomes for individuals. For example, in the United Kingdom, evaluation is being undertaken on the Work and Health Programme to determine whether it is possible for government to provide services as effectively as third party providers (DWP, 2021[7]). This type of analysis can shed more insight into the precise delivery challenges and how to optimally deliver policy.

Figure 2.6. Cost of programme provision varies significantly by region

Average cost of programme provision by programme type and region

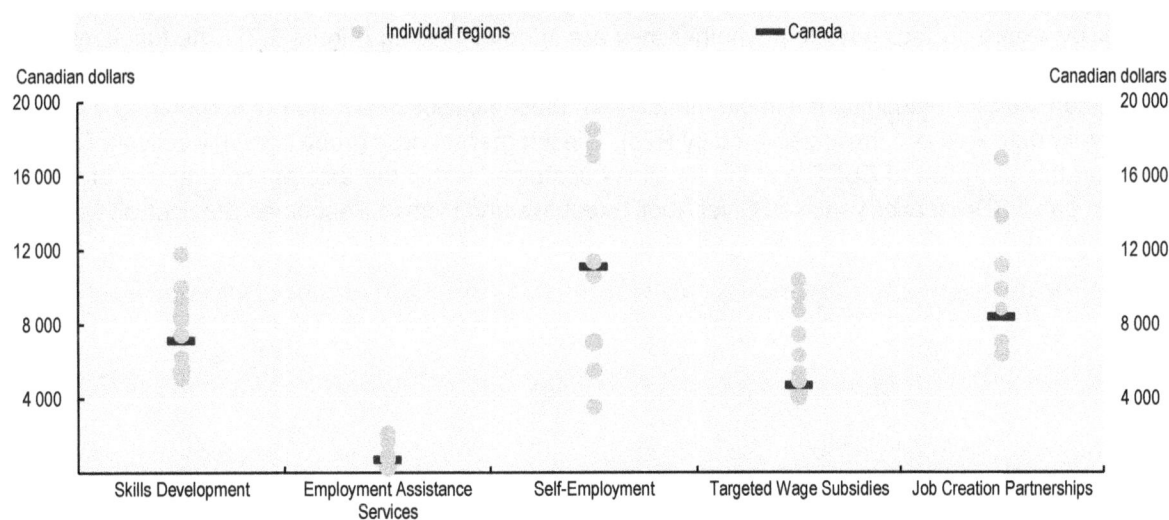

Note: Average cost per participant 2002-05. Individual provinces and territories (PTs) estimates are extracted from the PTs report. Canada is taken from the aggregate report on Canada.
Source: Individual Employment and Social Development Canada (ESDC) impact assessment reports on provinces and territories (2017-2018), available at www.canada.ca.

StatLink https://stat.link/vfckx3

2.4. ESDC's analytical structure

Conducting analytical research on the LMDAs involves the co-ordination and co-operation of a broad set of staff within the ministry. Planning analysis, allocating resources, accessing data and working with PTs mean that an extensive network of interactions and governance is required, to ensure the smooth and efficient conduct of work that is vital to understanding how ALMPs help individuals into work. This section reviews how those resources are organised in ESDC to conduct analysis.

ESDC is a large federal government ministry, headed up by four government ministers and five deputy ministers. Its broad remit is to "build a stronger and more inclusive Canada, to support Canadians in helping them live productive and rewarding lives and to improve Canadians' quality of life" (ESDC, 2018[8]). This covers responsibility for pensions, unemployment insurance, student and apprentice loans, education savings and wage earner protection programmes and passport services. How any ministry organises itself has implications on the functioning of its programmes and services. This section reviews how ESDC organises the functions that relate to evaluation of its ALMPs and how the teams that do this interact with wider departments and services. It also reviews how this has changed over time. Setting this information out up front will provide a framework with which to contextualise some of the details explored further in the report.

2.4.1. ESDC separates out evaluation from the teams responsible for policy development

The division into external and internally facing groups means that not all of the responsibility for a particular programme lies within the same chain of command. For evaluation work in ESDC, this means that teams that conduct the work, for example on the LMDA, do not sit in the same group or directorates as the one with policy and implementation responsibility for them. The organisation of evaluation sits within a broader federal requirement, via the Treasury Board "Policy on Results", to implement and maintain a neutral evaluation function.

ESDC broadly organises itself into two groups, determined by whether the function of the underlying branch is to deliver externally facing work or whether they are internally facing (Figure 2.7). The functions within the external group are focussed on the delivery of programmes, including responsibility for policy development and for managing the implementation of these policies in Canada (incorporating those that are federally delivered and those delivered by PTs). The internal services group primarily delivers functions to support the operation of ESDC and the functions contained within the external programme group. For example, pan-ESDC services such as Chief Audit Executive and Human Resources Services sit within this group.

Figure 2.7. The split of work into external and internal groups means policy spans different organisational jurisdictions

A view into the Skills and Employment and Service and Strategic Policy Branches

External Programmes	Internal Services
Skills and Employment Branch	**Service and Strategic Policy Branch**
Functions include: Policy and Implementation of Employment Insurance, ALMPs, Literacy and Skills	**Functions include:** Evaluation responsibility across ALMP and passive labour market policies, management of departmental administrative data
Directorates and Teams Include:	**Directorates** and Teams Include:

External Programmes	Internal Services	
Employment Program Policy and Design	**Evaluation Directorate**	**Chief Data Officer**
Labour Transfer Agreement Implementation	Statutory & Grants & Contribution Evaluation	Data Management
Workforce Development Agreements and Targeted Programs	Partnership Evaluation	Data Strategies & Development
Policy - Employment Insurance Part II and Labour Market Development Agreements	Strategic Planning & Methodology	Strategic Partnerships, Planning & Dissemination
Office of Literacy and Essential Skills		

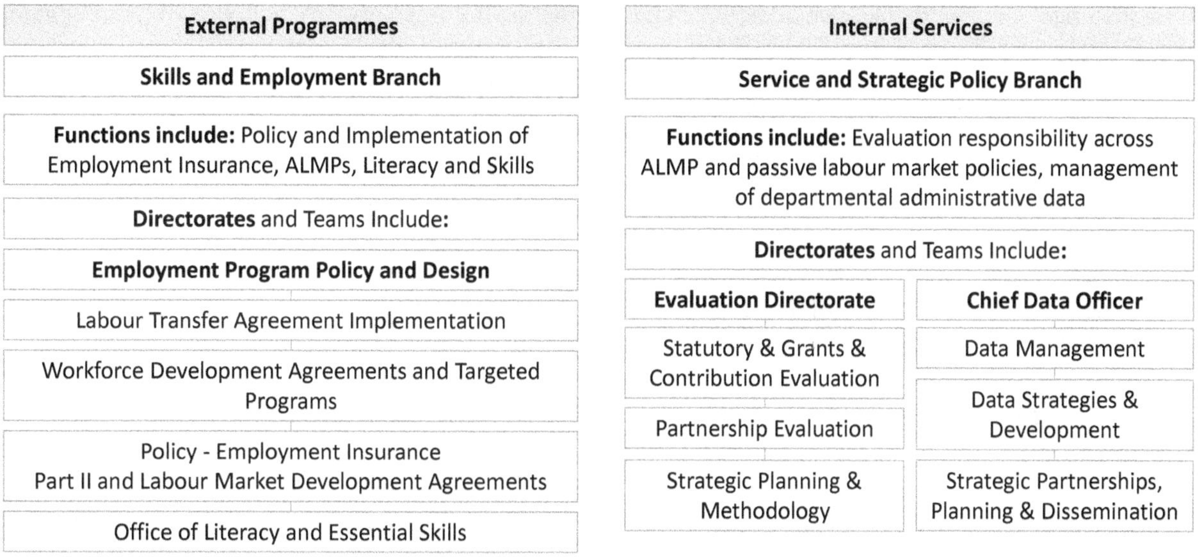

Note: Both Skills and Employment and Service and Strategic Policy Branches have more functions and directorates within them. This figure displays only those that concern the discussion of LMDA. Similarly, the External Programmes group includes; Income Security and Social Development Branch, Office of Disability Issues, Learning Branch, Program Operations Branch, Skills and Employment Branch, Office of Literacy and Essential Skills. The Internal Services group includes; Chief Audit Executive, Chief Financial Officer, Corporate Secretary, Human Resources Services Branch, Innovation, Information and Technology Branch, Legal Services Branch, Public Affairs and Stakeholder Relations Branch, Strategic and Service Policy Branch.

Source: ESDC organisational charts, https://www.canada.ca/en/employment-social-development/corporate/organizational-structure.html.

The Strategic and Service Policy branch delivers functions related to ALMP analysis and data storage

The Strategic and Service Policy Branch integrates strategic and operational policy and service delivery across ESDC. Its responsibilities include the development of economic, social and service strategic policies related to the mandate of the department and it conducts research activities in these areas. It has responsibility for the strategic management of data, for programme evaluation and for intergovernmental and international relations.[4] The evaluation function in ESDC exists as a directorate, the Evaluation Directorate, within this branch, as does the Chief Data Officer (CDO) directorate.

Within the evaluation directorate there are three separate divisions covering statutory and grants and contributions evaluation, partnership evaluation and strategic planning and methodology.

The LMDA evaluations are conducted by staff within the partnership evaluation and strategic planning and methodology divisions of this directorate.

The Skills and Employment branch is responsible for policy and programme delivery

The Skills and Employment branch provides programmes and initiatives that promote skills development, labour market participation and inclusiveness, as well as programmes ensuring labour market efficiency. This branch includes the employment programme policy and design directorate. Within this directorate there are divisions that have responsibility for the implementation of the LMTAs, Labour Market Transfer Targeted Programs, and policy on employment insurance benefits and support measures (ALMPs). A data and systems team is responsible for the LMDAs and WDAs data upload, quality and integrity of these data, and documenting data changes over time, is also situated within this directorate.

This corporate structure means that the two different branches of the organisation have to collaborate to bring together policy development and evidence. If corporate organisation was wholly aligned by policy area, then evaluation and policy would sit within the same area (for example, LMDA policy, implementation and evaluation would fall under the same directorate).

The current organisation brings both benefits and challenges. The benefits of a centralised evaluation function within ESDC, mean that it is easier to co-ordinate evaluations, ensure the neutrality of the function, share expertise and gain through a coalescence of that expertise in a specific area. The challenge is then to ensure that priorities are aligned with the policy and implementation of the specific work area and that evaluation and evidence are properly brought to bear within that policy domain. Duplication of work needs to be constantly reviewed. Separate analytical teams exist within the policy and programme divisions. If there is not careful co-ordination of respective remits and priorities, it may mean that teams do similar work or overlap in function, reducing the efficiency of the analytical resources deployed.

2.4.2. Teams within the evaluation directorate are defined by function to increase specialisation

The successful delivery of analytical impact assessments of ALMPs over the years has helped the evaluation function in ESDC embed itself as a central part of the policy making process. In recent years, the evaluation directorate has increasingly relied on conducting evaluation internally rather than relied on costly external contracts. This shift allowed the directorate to increase its workforce from around 50 staff in 2013 to about 70 in 2021 while maintaining the same overall level of resources allocated to the evaluation function. Furthermore, this shift allowed it to take on more and varied activities to support policy making within the Department and also to further develop specialised teams within the directorate itself.

Broadly the three main functional areas for evaluation are:

- Data preparation (Strategic Planning and Methodology Division) – This area became particularly important prior to the move from survey based analyses to administrative data based analyses. It was the catalyst for that move and remains an integral part of the analytical set-up. This ensures the data provided by CDO are turned into the requisite analytical files for analysis. Extensive data documentation has been produced to ensure business continuity.

- Impact analysis (Strategic Planning and Methodology Division) – These teams work directly with the data to apply the statistical techniques needed to produce estimates of programme impacts. The specialisation of these teams allow them to focus on ensuring they are applying the most rigorous and up-to-date techniques to interrogate the data, without having to dilute as much expertise on data assimilation and preparation.

- Liaison with PTs and qualitative analysis (Partnerships Evaluation Division) – A vital part of the whole analytical process is to liaise with PTs to discuss issues and jointly plan evaluation work. Without this function, the whole process would be untenable. Planning and conducting contextual qualitative analysis to supplement the quantitative impact assessment is important to provide PTs with insight into what works in their province or territory and why.

Increased resource has allowed further specialisation

Following the swift towards the internal conduct of quantitative evaluation activities, the resources available for methodology and data as part of the Evaluation Directorate increased from three people in 2015 to about 10 in 2021. This has allowed them to expand work areas (for example, starting to conduct gender based evaluation) but has also enabled increased specialisation. Dedicated functions have now been carved out for methodology (advising on the tools and techniques to use for impact assessment and providing quality assurance protocols to follow) and data development (turning the data provided by CDO into analytical datasets that are ready to be used for impact assessments, ensuring that comprehensive data documentation and meta-data exist to support their use).

In-house delivery of counterfactual impact evaluation, which started with the LMDAs, has since expanded to the former Youth Employment Strategy as well as the Aboriginal Skills and Employment Training Strategy and the objective is to include the Workforce Development Agreements. The previously outlined split of responsibility, so that the evaluation function is centralised and conducts all of these evaluations in the same directorate, means that organisation, prioritisation and resource considerations can be managed in one division. The challenge is to reach consensus on priorities between the evaluation director and directors of policy and implementation, who sit in different areas of the department.

2.4.3. The establishment of a separate Chief Data Officer function helps to support evaluation

An important element to support the evaluation teams in conducting their work is the separation of the corporate function that deals with data management, data transformation and integration, development, procurement and dissemination. This organisation also brings benefits to other analytical teams, as it creates a coherent and consistent structure and direction around data management and use to analysts.

The Chief Data Officer (CDO) role was created in 2016 in order to lead the implementation of an enterprise-wide data strategy focused on unlocking the business value of its data assets while protecting the privacy and security of its clients. The enterprise strategy brings a horizontal perspective to ESDC's management and use of data, empowering data users with the right knowledge, tools and supports, creating several advantages for ESDC, and specifically for evaluation:

- Provides a central point of contact for data transfer requests, streamlining interactions and ensuring a common standard for transfer. In the context of LMDA this ensures that all provincial data are managed and processed according to the same set of rules.
- It has created common data access protocols for data users, ensuring consistency of use and enhancing protection of data privacy and security.
- Progress has been made in improving access to properly contextualised and curated data, including the introduction of a web-based portal for access requests, and the establishment of a Data Foundations Programme to deliver the enterprise data infrastructure to enable secure and timely access to high quality data (including a data catalogue, enterprise data warehouse, and a data lake).
- Teams within the CDO directorate process, transform, standardise and clean data to make it easier to use for users and create common files for data usage.
- Fosters collaboration and data stewardship, breaking down silos and encouraging partnerships to maximise the responsible and ethical use of data and tools and methods for analysis (e.g. machine learning, advanced analytics) across the policy to service continuum (from policy analysis and research, through to service delivery, evaluation and reporting)

2.4.4. Relationships function well between federal government and PTs

LMDA delivery and evaluation of ALMPs is the responsibility of PTs. Federally conducting the evaluation element within ESDC (jointly with PTs) therefore requires extensive communication, excellent organisation and collaborative leadership. The relationship between the federal level and PTs in this context is reported to be harmonious and filled with trust. Formal governance procedures and honest and accountable leadership have been cited as laying the foundations for this relationship.

The governance procedures in place ensure that all parties get a voice in proceedings (all PTs have an equal vote, so it means there is no size bias in terms of PTs with larger populations having greater influence) and the work plans developed are based on mutually agreed outcomes. There is an Evaluation Steering Committee with representatives from all participating PTs and federal officials, which decides on all matters relating to evaluation of the LMDA at a working level.

The Forum of Labour Market Ministers, created in 1983, provides a forum for ministers from federal, provincial and territorial levels to discuss high-level issues relating to the overall labour market policies and strategies, of which evaluations is one. Its various working groups also allow for information sharing and discussion of issues between PTs and federal officials. This ensures that any issues arising from the evaluation work can be discussed further among senior policy makers.

An important element within this dynamic has been the value of the quantitative analysis in helping to make the case with PTs that they could also benefit from projects led by ESDC with their collaboration. For example, research that proved the value of early interventions with jobseekers (Handouyahia et al, 2014[9]) was considered instrumental in securing broad agreement among PTs on the value of collection of good quality data, so that proper evaluation could be conducted on policy delivery.

Officials from PTs are also grateful for the opportunities that these formal face-to-face channels provide for more informal networking and peer learning among each other. That these processes have been suspended somewhat as a consequence of COVID-19 means that there is less of an opportunity than was previously the case. It will be important to re-establish these once sanitary circumstances allow, so that PTs can continue this process of peer learning.

2.4.5. Canada delivers a suite of ALMPs that are underpinned by evidence generated by internally delivered analysis

In conclusion, Canada has a range of ALMPs to support its jobseekers find better work, primarily orientated around employment support services and training to improve skills. However, funding for this has been eroded over the years and Canada spends less than its OECD counterparts. ESDC has established an evidence base that its policies are effective and deliver value for money for the taxpayer, but evidence shows that there is variation to this geographically and among different groups of individuals. Much of this evidence has been generated using internal analysis, with resource that it has built over the years. In line with federal policy guiding the internal conduct of performance measurement and evaluation, ESDC's evaluation function is centralised within the ministry and it sits outside of the policy and programme teams that manage the implementation of the policy. This ensures the neutrality of the function and provides an opportunity to benefit from collective expertise controlled within the same directorate, so that work priorities can be aligned. For instance, the evaluations on the former Youth Employment Skills Strategy as well as the Aboriginal Skills and Employment Training strategy benefit from being conducted by the same teams within the evaluation directorate. As they use the same underlying data to produce the evaluations,[5] this reduces the need for duplication in expertise if separate teams were to conduct them instead. The expansion of data resources and the establishment of a Chief Data Office in ESDC has also allowed the department to streamline and adopt a strategic approach to data management, facilitating data access across the department and further allowing the evaluation teams to focus on the quantitative analysis. An established system of governance and forums for exchange has facilitated ESDC's ability to conduct these evaluations jointly with PTs.

References

DWP (2021), *Work and Health Progamme statistics: background information and methodology*, Department for Work & Pensions, United Kingdom, https://www.gov.uk/government/publications/work-and-health-programme-statistics-background-information-and-methodology/work-and-health-progamme-statistics-background-information-and-methodology (accessed on 20 December 2021).
[7]

ESDC (2021), *2019/2020 Employment Insurance Monitoring and Assessment Report*, Employment and Social Development Canada, http://www12.esdc.gc.ca/sgpe-pmps/p.5bd.2t.1.3ls@-eng.jsp?pid=72896.
[1]

ESDC (2020), *Evaluation of the Aboriginal Skills and Employment Training Strategy and the SKills and Partnership Fund*, Employment and Social Development Canada, https://www.canada.ca/en/employment-social-development/corporate/reports/evaluations/aboriginal-skills-employment-training-strategy-skills-partnership-fund.html.
[2]

ESDC (2020), *Hoizontal Evaluation of the Youth Employment Strategy: Career Focus Stream*, Employment and Social Development Canada, https://www.canada.ca/en/employment-social-development/corporate/reports/evaluations/horizontal-career-focus.html.
[3]

ESDC (2020), *Horizontal Evaluation of the Youth Employment Strategy: Skills Link Stream*, Employment and Social Development Canada, https://www.canada.ca/en/employment-social-development/corporate/reports/evaluations/horizontal-skills-link.html.
[4]

ESDC (2018), *Employment and Social Development Canada 2017/18 Departmental Results Report*, Employment and Social Development Canada, https://www.canada.ca/en/employment-social-development/corporate/reports/departmental-results/2017-2018.html.
[8]

ESDC (2017), *Evaluation of the Labour Market Development Agreements: Synthesis Report*, Employment and Social Development Canada, https://publications.gc.ca/site/eng/9.841271/publication.html.
[6]

Handouyahia et al (2014), *Effects of the timing of participation in employment assistance services : technical study prepared under the second cycle for the evaluation of the labour market development agreements*, Employment and Social Development Canada, https://publications.gc.ca/site/eng/9.834560/publication.html.
[9]

OECD (2021), *Labour Market Programmes Database*, https://stats.oecd.org//Index.aspx?QueryId=112084.
[5]

Notes

[1] The Indigenous Skills and Employment Training was formerly called The Aboriginal Skills and Employment Training. The Youth Employment and Skills Strategy was formerly The Youth Employment Strategy. Both of the referenced papers assessed the programmes under their old names.

[2] This report refers to ESDC even where its functions may have been undertaken by a predecessor ministry prior to its formation.

[2] Not including programme administration. Some PTs will finance programmes directly from this budget, for example internally delivered EAS

[3] Using OECD LMP database categories 11: Placement and related services, 20: Training, 40: Employment incentives, 50: Sheltered and supported employment and rehabilitation, 60: Direct job creation, 70: Start-up incentives as the denominator, and categories 11 and 20 for the numerator. Data are based on 2019. Except for New Zealand and Australia for whom 2019 data are affected by the onset of COVID-19 and 2018 data are used.

[4] https://www.canada.ca/en/employment-social-development/corporate/organizational-structure.html.

[5] The WDAS is conducted separately using survey data, due to current limitations on the administrative data available.

3 Leveraging administrative data for analysis

Rich and comprehensive data are essential to conduct high-quality impact evaluations. Over the years, Employment and Social Development Canada (ESDC) has moved from using expensively collected survey data to utilising its register data on employment insurance and Provinces and Territories (PTs) data on participation in active labour market policies. Integrating these data directly with Canada Revenue Agency data on income has been essential to assess high-quality data on outcomes. ESDC analysis could benefit even further by enriching these data with more socio-economic information from other agencies and PTs. Facilitating greater access to data to make it easier for external researchers to conduct analysis would encourage further innovation and provide more evidence on how policies work to help individuals secure good jobs.

3.1. Introduction

Data are critical to the success of impact evaluations of policy. Without rich and robust data any inference from analysis is likely to be limited and estimates inaccurate. Analytical data requirements are different depending on the technique being used. When participation in programmes is randomised and the accuracy of the estimator is assured through the randomisation, little more is required than accurate data on programme participation and on the outcome variables in question to estimate programme impacts. Observational studies, such as those involving regression analysis or matching, rely on having a rich set of data on personal characteristics to ensure individuals compared are alike. There are nuances within this; if evaluators want to look at specific groups within the population, even a randomised study may require richer data on personal characteristics.

Typically, those studies that do not rely on the evaluator's ability to control selection into the programme are more data hungry than those that do. ESDC's primary methodology for impact assessment is non-experimental therefore placing a greater burden on data needs to ensure unbiased estimates. Over the years, ESDC has moved away from collection of these data using surveys of participants and non-participants, which were expensive, cumbersome to administer and did not inform income well, to make use of the rich set of information that they possess in their administrative data. Key in this process is linking the ESDC and PT administrative data to Canada Revenue Agency (CRA) data on income. This has permitted ESDC to make a thorough, comprehensive and accurate account of post-participation outcomes for individuals.

As technology progresses and data collection and storage is facilitated, countries are making strides in the collection and assimilation of different administrative data to aid policy analysis and make data more widely available (OECD, 2020[1]). Many countries are moving towards more open data access to allow external researchers secure access to data in order to benefit from more widespread access to the expertise needed to interrogate them. Statistics Canada, Canada's federal statistics agency, acts as a repository for administrative and survey data for non-government researchers. However, at present it is not possible to access all of the data required to conduct impact evaluation of active labour market policies (ALMPs). Opening access further would democratise these evaluations, helping innovation and providing useful cross-validation of ESDC analysis.

3.2. The pathway towards linked administrative data

When the Labour Market Development Agreements (LMDAs) were launched in 1996, funding was transferred to provinces and territories (PTs) to deliver ALMPs. It came with a stipulation to conduct evaluation of their delivery. Twelve out of the thirteen PTs agreed to conduct this evaluation jointly with ESDC (and its predecessors). This change meant that data were now required to be collected separately from each PTs, who were responsible for their own administration of the LMDAs, so that ESDC could conduct the evaluation jointly with them. The biggest challenge here was the collection of high-quality data on outcomes.

At the same time, data linking between ministries was not routine at the inception of the LMDAs, which meant it was not possible for ESDC to observe earnings data for participants and non-participants, by integrating participants' data with income data from Canada Revenue Agency (CRA). Therefore a decision was taken to utilise surveys to collect data on outcomes and programme participation. Because the evaluations were being delivered for each of the separate PTs, this meant a separate provincial survey was required for each jurisdiction. For the first cycle of evaluation, which took until 2012 to complete, information was gathered in this way. The nature of the collection meant that progress was slow, as it was a resource intensive process to manually interview individuals and record information from them. It meant that only two to three provincial studies could be conducted simultaneously and it took around ten years for the first cycle of analysis to be completed covering all participating PTs.

3.2.1. The shift towards evaluation driven by administrative data

The cumbersome nature and cost of individual surveys for PTs, led ESDC officials to explore the possibility of utilising administrative data to conduct the evaluations. Government administrative data offer several advantages in their use for impact assessment, relative to other forms of data such as survey, or privately held data:

- Universal Coverage – all recipients of government benefits are recorded as clients. They do not suffer from attrition – individuals have their details recorded for the duration of their claim. This contrasts to survey data where individuals may opt-out of follow-up data collection.
- Accuracy – they are not subject to recall errors. Individuals do not have to remember how much they are paid or when, or what programme they were participating in.
- Precision – they have the benefit of scale. Being population data, every individual is covered, so sample sizes are large. This aids statistical precision, which is beneficial where the outcomes of interest have a lot of natural variation (for example earnings), the expected impacts of the policy are small (for example in job counselling services), there are relatively few people participating in the programme or where the researcher wants to look at impacts for sub-groups. It means there can be greater confidence of detecting an impact where one exists.
- Timeliness – they are often timely, since they exist to support benefit administration, details need to be captured in real time.
- Cost – relative to other forms of data collection (such as surveys), they are cheap to collect because they are already collected for benefit administration purposes

These factors all contributed towards the move by ESDC to utilise their administrative data for evaluation. With appropriate privacy provisions in place, approval was granted in 2004 to integrate ESDC data to CRA data on income and tax. On this basis, ESDC started to evaluate the scope for administrative data to replace survey data for the impact analysis. This work started by comparing the CRA data to the survey data collected in one province. It revealed that ALMP participants systematically over reported their income and non-participants systematically under-reported it. The presence of this difference in "mis-reporting" meant that programme estimates based on these data would overstate the impact of the programme on earnings. These results paved the way for the systematic adoption of administrative data to replace survey data in the second round of LMDA evaluation, starting in 2010. CRA administrative data on income could replace the income data collected from the surveys and a combination of administrative data on past benefit receipt from ESDC and past income data from CRA could replace the socio-economic data collected, which was used to compare similar participants and non-participants.

An additional benefit from the adoption of administrative data was the considerable cost saving to government on offer. The bilateral provincial surveys were expensive- around CAD 1 million per annum was spent on putting surveys into the field (Gingras et al., 2017[2]), with the associated data collection and assimilation. The use of CRA data combined with ALMP participation data was exploiting data already held for administrative purposes. Initial work by analysts to interrogate, assimilate and compile the data into a format conducive to analysis was completed and then ongoing maintenance and administration costs are minimal, compared to the costs associated with individual survey data collection at the PTs level.

3.3. Building a data platform for evaluation

In order to provide a platform to conduct their quantitative analysis, the ESDC evaluation directorate have developed the Labour Market Program Data Platform (LMPDP) (Table 3.1 (ESDC, 2020[3])). This platform consists of 11 separate but relationally integrated data entities which enable analysts to look at:

- Patterns of actual participation in ALMPs;
- Patterns of eligibility to participate in ALMPs;
- Patterns of claiming employment insurance benefits;
- Annual sources of income;
- Annual job patterns.

The process of compiling this platform takes three stages:

1. In the first phase, ESDC administrative data on ALMP participation are compiled. These data are taken from four separate sources, which come from different administrative systems within ESDC. For example, participants in programmes in the former Youth Employment Strategy are held in a different system than those participants in Labour Market Development Agreement (LMDA) programmes. Important data cleaning is conducted in this stage, to ensure that data are chronologically consistent and participation in different programmes is not in conflict (for example, individuals are not participating in two ALMPs at the same time where this is not possible).

2. In the second phase, the PTs data on programme participation are merged with ESDC data on employment insurance. This allows eligible non-participants to be identified. Because participation in the LMDA is contingent on qualifying contributions to employment insurance, this stage is important to reconcile how participation relates to periods of qualification. The employment insurance data also contain a number of personal characteristics (such as age, gender, marital status, disability) that are brought in, so they can be used for later analysis to compare participants with similar non-participants. In order to create a control group of individuals that did not participate in an ALMP, the detailed history of individuals must be analysed to check for underlying entitlement to participation. By doing this, ESDC can then compare individuals who did not participate in an ALMP, but who were eligible to do so, with those that did participate.

3. In the third phase, added to the ALMP participation (phase 1 dataset) and timing data (phase 2 dataset) are data on annual income and social assistance receipt from CRA and information on job spells. The CRA data are updated annually and transferred to ESDC. This step makes it possible to observe work outcomes of both participants and non-participants. An important step in this stage of the data preparation is the simulation of participation among eligible non-participants.

Constructing this platform provides ESDC several advantages. The first is that they have a consistent platform for evaluation. Evaluations of the LMDA, Youth and Indigenous programmes have been conducted using the same data platform. This creates:

- Efficiency – raw data are not being re-processed for every new evaluation.
- Consistency – the participation data and related income and employment records are the same for individuals across evaluations.
- Institutional knowledge – having an enduring platform that analysts use also means that expertise that is built up on the data can easily be shared among ESDC analysts, meaning quality assurance is easier and analysis can be conducted quickly.

An extensive suite of data documentation and metadata has been amassed to ensure that ESDC has business continuity and that new staff are able to quickly assimilate themselves with the data. The existence of a data team within the evaluation directorate has helped to ensure that data are well documented, allowing for analysis to be conducted correctly and maintaining consistency between analysis on different projects.

Table 3.1. There are three stages to data processing to build the Labour Market Program Data Platform

Phase	Input Data	Data Processing	Output Data
1	-Input datasets on ALMP participation start and end date - Four separate datasets covering participation in ALMPs under different funding streams - Participation in ALMPs (start and end dates, programme type) related to eligibility through EI contributions	- Consolidate data to fix inconsistencies and incompatibilities - Imputation of end dates when missing or invalid - Remove duplicates/redundancies - Normalise coding and record structure	**Integrated Intervention File**
2	**Integrated intervention File** Employment Insurance (EI) data - Receipt/amount and spell data on EI -Individual Characteristics (for example, age, gender, marital status, disability)	- Calculate timing and duration of participation in ALMPs relative to EI qualifying periods (e.g. how many weeks after the start of EI receipt does someone participate in ALMPs) - Develop timing and duration models so that periods of eligibility are constructed to compare non-participants to participant	**Timing and Duration File**
3	**Integrated intervention File** **Timing and Duration File** Canada Revenue Agency annual tax return data – incorporates both income data and data on social assistance Receipt Record of Employment – records on job separation containing employment information	- Integrate Administrative Datasets - Simulate participation among eligible non-participants - Creation of analytical variables for data platform (for example, earnings pre- and post-participation and derived variables such as skill level)	**LABOUR MARKET PROGRAM DATA PLATFORM**

Source: ESDC (2021[4]), Labour Market Program Data Platform – Data Dictionary v3.05a; Handouyahia (2019[5]), "The creation of a rich data platform to support net impact evaluation of Labour Market Programmes", https://www.oecd.org/employment/emp/S4.5.%20Handouyahia_CAN.pdf.

3.3.1. Securely linking administrative datasets enables a comprehensive analysis of outcomes

Linking together administrative datasets on Employment Insurance with CRA tax return data enables ESDC to look at a comprehensive suite of outcome information on individuals (rather than just patterns of employment insurance receipt), which is much richer than if ESDC administrative data were used alone.

Canada has a mixed ability to integrate its different administrative data together, driven in part by its federal structure. Similar to the majority of OECD countries, it is able to link its employment register with its unemployment register. However, it is one of only seven countries for which its social assistance register is held at a regional level (OECD, 2020[1]). Whilst these regional files are shared with ESDC, in principle this may cause additional costs to employ those data in the LMPDP as they would require inspection, standardisation and collation. However, the use of CRA tax returns facilitates the easy incorporation of this information since social assistance amounts received in a given calendar year are included on these returns (though these data are only available for employment insurance recipients and LMDA participants). The incorporation of the CRA data into the LMPDP then means that ESDC can evaluate not only the impact of its programmes on receipt of employment insurance, but also on social assistance and on earnings from work.

The principle drawback, relative to other OECD countries with employment register data, is the lack of information on employment spells in the employment register. It is one of only three countries for whom there is no information contained within that register (OECD, 2020[1]). These data are recorded in the Record of Employment dataset available in ESDC, but they are not always reliable and are only issued on separation for a job, so it is not possible to identify spells of employment that have not yet ended. However, they are a mandatory piece of information for individuals claiming Employment Insurance, so consideration could be given on whether to analyse them in the evaluation of current employment insurance claimants. Improving the coverage of these data would permit further insight into the outcomes of jobseekers.

Data are pseudo-anonymised to comply with data protection regulation

Data are protected and integrated together using identifier keys. Social Insurance numbers are used to link participants, but have been encrypted by an algorithm so that the key is no longer the same as the original and is instead replaced by a unique "sequence key". In this way, with the same encryption across datasets, it is possible to link individuals without ever disclosing their actual social security numbers. Names and addresses of individuals are removed so that no personal information remains.

Access and linking of these data sources is dependent on approval from the Privacy and Information Security Committee (PISC) review and Deputy Minister Approval. CRA data are updated annually and brought into ESDC's secure data warehouse and are controlled using business cases, where named individuals have to specify their business reason for accessing the data and agree to abide by the security procedures in place for data access.

3.3.2. Socio-demographic and past outcomes data provide rich information on individuals

The data that ESDC integrates into the LMPDP provide them with rich information on socio-demographic characteristics on labour market participants, which are critical to conducting counterfactual impact evaluations (the significance of this is discussed in Chapter 4). One of the drawbacks to administrative data is that they are often relatively sparse. Ministries can be limited in their ability to collect only the data they need for administration of benefits. Data on personal characteristics of claimants can be lacking. When conducting impact assessments having rich data on socio-economic status, educational history, marital status, motivations and aspirations, is pivotal to explaining an individual's choices (Heckman, Lalonde and Smith, 1999[6]; Lechner and Wunsch, 2013[7]), particularly with respect to the labour market. Many of these variables will not be available to a ministry that deals with administration of unemployment insurance, as they are not necessary to discharge these duties. However, this sparseness of administrative data can be mitigated by using detailed historic information on outcomes. Things like education and motivation are highly correlated to earnings, so by using information on past outcomes and benefit receipt it is possible to proxy these variables, even where they are not recorded directly. ESDC records and uses a full five years of past employment outcomes and benefit receipt to help ensure that this information is rich. This permits ESDC to create a detailed typology of claimants, proxying for other unobserved variables.

The socio-demographic and historic earnings and benefit data contained in the LMPDP provide a strong basis for which to compare alike individuals that did and did not participate in ALMPs. ESDC makes use of up to 75 socio-demographic and labour market variables, which are observed over five years prior to the participation period (ESDC, 2017[8]). The data include information on a range of characteristics that are used for the evaluation work (Table 3.2). Particularly important within this set of data are "past outcomes" – looking at the earnings and receipt of employment insurance and social assistance for five years prior to the period in question.

The main additional socio-economic variables captured in the LMPDP are age, gender, marital status, industry and occupation of previous job, and self-reported characteristics such as whether belonging to an identifiable "visible minority", being Indigenous or having a disability. The majority of this information comes from the employment insurance administrative data and is collected as part of the administration of that benefit. Marital status is contained on the CRA income tax data. These variables are useful both to disaggregate programme impacts for different groups, and to construct groups of similar participants and non-participants.

Table 3.2. Variables used by ESDC in the statistical analysis

Variables		
Age	Gender	Aboriginal origin
Visible minority	Disability	Marriage
Skill levels – Five groups based on occupation codes (managerial occupations where factors other than education is important, occupations requiring a university degree, college/vocational/apprenticeship, high school (one to four years of secondary schooling) or occupational (up to two years), on-the-job training (up to two years secondary school and short work demonstration))	Province/territory of claim	Industry of previous job (NAICS 2-digit code)
Number of hours of work contributing to employment insurance entitlement	Reason for previous job separation	Whether a new job market entrant
Year and quarter of ALMP participation (or eligible participation for non-participants)	Gap between start date of employment insurance receipt and start date of ALMP participation	Number of weeks with earnings between commencement of employment insurance receipt and start date (potential start date for non-participants) in ALMP
Participation in employment programmes in the previous five years	Annual earnings in the previous five years	Annual amount received in employment insurance (EI) or social assistance (SA) in the previous five years

Source: Authors summary of ESDC (2019[9]), Quantitative Methodology Report – Final; ESDC (2021[10]), "Analysis of Employment Benefits and Support Measures (EBSM) Profile and Medium-Term Incremental Impacts from 2010 to 2017, Technical Report, 2021".

The absence of data on education and family status means some sub-group analysis is not possible

At the time that ESDC put the LMPDP together, it did not possess information on individuals who had children. Whilst CRA tax returns do record the presence of children for whom a non-refundable tax credit may be claimed, it appears only on the tax record of the parent with the highest income (ESDC, 2019[9]). In Canada, the propensity for women to provide childcare to children at home means these issues are likely to disproportionately affect them. They spend almost 26 hours per week more than men caring for children (Statistics Canada, 2021[11]). Details on the presence and age of children would allow a much more detailed understanding of how ALMPs may influence parents' labour market participation decisions. This is particularly pertinent at different points in children's ages, for example when they start or leave school. This may be achieved via the incorporation of extra data. For example CRA data on child benefit receipt might allow some of these issues to be surmounted. These data incorporate the number of dependent children and because records exist for every year of receipt, it would be possible to broadly proxy ages of children by looking at the start date of benefit receipt and changes to the number of dependent children over time.

Similarly data to accurately compare young ALMP participants to non-participants are sparse. ESDC does not hold information on educational attainment for all individuals. Information is held on self-reported educational attainment for participants in ALMPs, but none is held for non-participants, meaning it cannot be used for the evaluation analysis. The reliance on past labour market and benefit receipt to proxy unobserved information on socio-economic status or education history, is unlikely to be completely sufficient for young people. As ESDC defines young people as aged 30 or under and given that relatively few of their customers have tertiary education (and so would have fewer schools years at older ages) (ESDC, 2021[10]), it is not likely that these issues dominate the results ESDC reports for this group. But, it does limit the ability to say with any certainty what the impact of these programmes may be for individuals that are relatively early on in their careers. This may have less impact on the LMDA evaluations because their catchment group requires some history of employment insurance (and therefore earnings) meaning it is unlikely to incorporate as many young people just leaving education, but may be more relevant to other programmes, such as the Youth Employment and Skills Strategy. Data on educational attainment can also be used as an outcome variable, which can be particularly useful for programmes for which a successful outcome might be that the participant then completes further training. New Zealand's experience demonstrates that its administrative data on educational attainment is useful in both of these respects (de Boer and Ku, 2018[12]; 2018[13]), facilitating better matching but also providing useful information on how policies affect skills attainment. It links these data into its Integrated Data Infrastructure, making their use in analysis particularly easy. This data infrastructure is similar in design to the LMPDP employed in Canada.

As young individuals are particularly susceptible to the pernicious effects of shocks to the labour market, as has been demonstrated recently with the COVID-19 crisis (OECD, 2021[14]), demonstrating which programmes are the most effective at helping them improve their outcomes is especially important. This is true not only for labour market outcomes but also for participation in education, which is another potentially common outcome for young individuals. It is for this group of individuals, for whom socio-economic administrative data are most unlikely to remove heterogeneity between individuals that alternative data strategies would help to produce robust impact assessments. Randomising participation for young people, or using detailed survey data to collect rich socio-economic data, could alleviate the current issues and allow young participants and non-participants to be better compared to one another.

Finland offers a good example of where extensive administrative data are available for use in analysis, facilitating more robust evaluations and permitting greater sub-sample analysis. The data held by Statistics Finland include a vast array of variables including educational level and qualification field, marital status size of household, tenure type, number and age groups of children, socio-economic group, occupation, alongside employment and unemployment histories. (Statistics Finland, 2022[15]). Education data can be useful not only in the identification of impacts on young people, but also as a means to explore whether ALMPs offer differential impacts depending on the level of qualification of people (Aho et al., 2018[16]). The ability to control for family characteristics allow researchers to look at the dynamics of household formation on ALMP participation and outcomes.

3.3.3. Important choices need to be made on what is being assessed and for whom

ESDC does not assess the impacts of individual interventions (ALMPs) but rather combinations of them. This is because interventions are not always assigned on an individual basis but are co-ordinated with other interventions to jointly achieve labour market objectives for the participant. The joint assignment of individual interventions is referred to as an "action plan". However, because the "action plan" to which an intervention belongs is not consistently recorded in the various administrative data sources it is reconstructed for each participant by grouping interventions that take place within six months (specifically 183 days) of each other. Groups of interventions combined this way are referred to as "Action Plan Equivalents" (APEs). ESDC sought expert guidance and conducted a detailed data assessment to formulate the construction of these APE to reconcile for the missing administrative data.

ESDC then takes every APE and assign a principal ALMP to it, which is the longest intervention in that specific APE. For example, in an APE that contained both Skills Development and Job Creation Partnership, if the participant was in the former ALMP for the longest time, that APE would be labelled "Skills Development".

Table 3.3 shows the combinations of ALMPs that are contained within APE for the cycle two evaluation conducted. For example, the APE with a principle ALMP of Targeted Wage Subsidy also contained an average of 1.66 programmes of Employment Assistance Support (EAS), 0.01 of Self-Employment and Job Creation Partnership. The high average number of EAS contained is due to its short duration and prominence in ALMP delivery- all jobseekers start with counselling before moving on to other ALMPs.

Table 3.3. APE contain a mixture of ALMPs in addition to the principle programme

The composition of Action Plan Equivalents by their underlying ALMPs, active claimants, cycle two evaluation

Principle ALMP	Share in total	Average number of programme occurrences per APE				
		Skills Development	Targeted Wage Subsidy	Self-Employment	Job Creation Partnership	Employment Assistance Support
Skills Development	23%	**1.00**	0.03	0.01	0.01	1.00
Targeted Wage Subsidy	3%	0	**1.00**	0.01	0.01	1.66
Self-Employment	4%	0	0.01	**1.00**	0.01	1.44
Job Creation Partnership	1%	0	0.03	0.01	**1.00**	1.10
Employment Assistance Support- only	69%	0	0	0	0.00	**1.00**

Note: ALMPs: Active Labour Market Programmes. The table reports Action Plan Equivalents (APE) for Active Claimant.
Source: ESDC (2017), "Evaluation of the Labour Market Development Agreements – Synthesis Report" and ESDC (2016), Cost-Benefit Analysis of Employment Benefits and Support Measures.

StatLink ᴍᴤᴸ https://stat.link/b6c0w8

This is not problematic to the mechanics of an impact assessment – combining ALMPs in this way, ESDC will still be able to make robust estimates of an APE's effect on outcomes, but it does complicate the interpretation of results somewhat. It becomes much harder to evaluate the different programmes next to each other, because the programmes are not defined in isolation, but rather in these combinations. The exception to this is the "Employment Assistance Support – only" category, which has been defined such that it is the only APE which contains no other ALMPs.

Estimating impacts per individual programme, rather than combining them together as is done now, would permit a more straightforward comparison of relative effects. Although the existence of ALMPs outside of the principal ALMP are minimal and it seems unlikely that they would make a big impact to the estimates of the APE, their presence confuse the presentation of the individual ALMP. It is hard to reconcile that a "co-ordinated" action plan for an individual would have an element with, for example, both a wage subsidy and a job creation programme. More likely it seems this is an artefact of the data rule to categorise programmes within six months of each other as part of the same APE and therefore as part of the same evaluation package. The exception to this discussion is for EAS which one would expect most APE to contain given their nature as a gateway service and precursor to further support. An easy way to implement this, for presentational purposes, without having to change the underlying modelling, would be to subtract the weighted outcomes for the secondary ALMPs from the principle estimate (for example, if a Skills Development APE increased earnings by CAD 5 000 but also contained 0.5 Employment Assistance Support – a programme of which was estimated to increase earnings by CAD 1 000 – report earnings of CAD 4 500).

Participants are split into different groups according to their employment insurance status and underlying personal characteristics

There are two separate facets to how ESDC addresses potential differential impacts of ALMPs in the evaluation that merit discussion.

The first is, subsequent to the first cycle of evaluation, ESDC's split of participants into two distinct groups:

- Current Claimants – An individual with a current open claim to employment insurance at the time of participation in an ALMP.

- Former Claimants – An individual with no current employment insurance claim but who qualifies for participation in a programme on the LMDA because they have had an open claim in the last five years or have paid a minimum level of EI contributions in the past ten years.

ESDC makes this distinction because of the problem of identifying a potential comparison group for "former claimant" and "non-insured" participants. Because available data are insufficient to identify programme-eligible non-participants, only those who show up for "limited treatment" (i.e. EAS) under the "former" and "non-insured" streams can demonstrate their eligibility under these streams. While this approach yields "relative" rather than "net" programme effects, it allows for the selection of a statistically equivalent comparison group using quasi-experimental methodology.

In order to create a group of individuals to compare against for the former claimants, ESDC uses those former claimants accessing EAS only as a control group and compare them to those former claimants who participate in other ALMPs. In this way, this somewhat solves the motivation issue by comparing two sets of individuals that have both come forward for support.

Because of this, ESDC is unable to estimate the impact of EAS on former claimants. However, this re-framing of the control population in order to make a comparison for the other ALMPs is a clever use of the data ESDC holds in order to provide inference on this group. This has the drawback that it then becomes more difficult to compare results for former claimants against current claimants. However, by proceeding with APE reporting as suggested in the previous section, this issue could also be surmounted.

The second consideration on participant type is on splitting estimates into different groups of individuals, who may respond differently to the ALMPs that they participate in. This is an area in which ESDC has progressively built evidence and expanded its ambition. In the second cycle of evaluation, beyond the split into current and former claimants, individuals were split into sub-groups based on whether they were:

- Youth (aged below 30 years)
- Older workers (aged 55 years and older)
- Long-tenured workers (employment insurance contributions in at least seven of the previous ten years)

In the third cycle of evaluation this sub-group analysis was extended further to other groups of interest, to look at:

- Gender
- Indigenous status
- Persons with disabilities
- Persons identifying as being a "visible minority"
- Immigration status

By defining sub-groups in this manner and separating out the analysis, it is possible to derive programme impacts for these specific groups. As the number of participants in a group becomes smaller, it can be harder to identify an impact statistically, because the precision of the statistical tests depends on the number of observations in the group (having more observations means more precise estimates). However, one of the advantages of having administrative data is that these sample size issues are much more easily avoided. In this respect, administrative data have allowed ESDC to be more ambitious.

ESDC is now moving towards the use of machine-learning algorithms to extend this approach further. The sub-group analysis talked about previously was conducted by pre-specifying groups of interest and then evaluating the impact on them. To this extent, it relies on user choice of these groups beforehand, based on some kind of expert knowledge that differences may occur and be meaningful to analyse. Machine-learning automates this process and uses the data to discern whether differences in outcomes occur and for which groups. The advantage of this is that it is not reliant on a person to pre-define the groups (risking incomplete or irrelevant sub-group choice), but it comes with the risk that the types of group chosen are less well qualitatively defined and for which it may be difficult to make operational delivery choices about (for example, if the algorithm chooses men, with three years of recent work in a managerial profession, interspersed with six months of unemployment prior to that, it may be difficult for counsellors to identify and serve those customers differently in practice).

3.3.4. A comprehensive suite of outcome variables are used in analysis

ESDC utilise the information contained in the LMPDP to look at a number of outcomes for individuals (participants and non-participants) (ESDC, 2021[10]). These outcome variables are:

- Annual employment earnings (A)
- The incidence of employment (denoted by whether an individual has had a spell of employment in a year)
- Annual amount of employment insurance benefits paid (B)
- Annual number of weeks of employment insurance benefit paid
- The incidence of social assistance receipt (denoted by whether an individual has had a spell of social assistance in a year)
- Annual amount of social assistance paid (C)
- Dependence on income support (defined as (B+C)/(A+B+C))

This set of outcome variables allows a comprehensive assessment of the impact of a programme on a participants subsequent labour market outcomes. ESDC's administrative data on employment insurance and income tax data on social assistance allow a thorough assessment of the subsequent impact of the programme on the payment of benefits to participants. CRA data on income is essential in looking at how much individuals earn in their subsequent employment. The combination of both of these datasets included in LMPDP allows a thorough assessment of an individual's post-participation income, including both work and non-work spells.

Because these outcomes are derived from administrative data they are high quality – there is no non-response bias or recall error. Errors can still occur in register data but their order of magnitude is typically lower than the aforementioned errors in survey data (see Meyer, C Mok and Sullivan (2015[17]) for a United States discussion or Bellemare, Kyui and Lacroix (2021[18]) for a discussion relating to Canadian immigration and earnings). This was also corroborated in ESDC's past survey and administrative data comparison and gave ESDC a strong rationale to continue with administrative data as the main source of information for outcomes data.

But currently it is difficult to look at indicators of job quality such as job transitions, tenure length and contract type

One of the drawbacks of the current set of outcome variables is that they do not permit much insight into job quality, apart from earnings. The indicator for incidence of employment does not capture tenure – a job spell of one week would look identical to a job lasting for the full 52 weeks. Similarly there is not presently a way to identify the number of spells of employment, to look at job cycling. Some of this can be inferred by the impact on total employment earnings (an individual earning less in a year must either be working for less time or at a lower wage), but at present it is impossible to say which of these factors drives the result.

This limits the extent to which the analysis can identify low income individuals who frequently cycle into and out of work, compared to those with more stable employment history and with fewer but longer transitions between states. Given that participation in ALMPs is likely to be concentrated at the lower end of the income distribution, this could be an important distinction to make when looking at the selection pathways into employment programmes (see Andersson et al. (2013[19]) for an example of how data aggregation can change programme estimates). For example, a paper utilising Swiss unemployment register data and social security administration data on earnings analysed how benefit sanctions impacted upon subsequent earnings stability, by looking at spells of employment (Arni, Lalive and Van Ours, 2012[20]). The incorporation of such information would allow ESDC to investigate how their ALMPs influence job tenure. This could be done potentially using the Record of Employment data, at least for active employment insurance claimants, for whom there are better quality data.

Similarly without information on contract type, it is not possible to see whether the successful completion of an ALMP moves individuals towards securing jobs with more permanent employment contracts. A recent study from France demonstrates the value that having data on contract type can have on determining whether ALMPs impact the type and quality of job available (Algan, Crépon and Glover, 2020[21]). Twenty-four OECD countries can link these data directly from their employment register (OECD, 2020[1]), making the process much more routine for their incorporation into analysis. Having complete information on an individual's occupation that would allow it to be used as an outcome variable, would allow an investigation into whether individuals moved up the job ladder as a result of participation. The current Record of Employment data contain some broad information on type of contract, an extension of these categories, to capture this information, may permit its incorporation into analysis.

Earnings data suffer from a lack of timeliness and aggregation which may inhibit policy makers

The use of CRA data for income and social assistance highlights the drawbacks of using administrative tax data, namely its timeliness and periodicity. The data held by ESDC on income and tax lag its ALMP programme data by two years. As individuals typically have to submit annual tax returns, the deadlines for which are some months after the end of the tax year, it means that there is a long lag to assimilate data. In the analysis of employment programmes, where the impacts of a programme can take some months to occur (for example, a training programme may last six months and then analysis should allow time for people to enter the labour market) this combination may mean that it is not practicable to evaluate policy until some years after its implementation. The lag in timely tax and income data is not a problem for policy analysis per se but, it does constrain policy makers in the shorter term, which may make a difference when budgets are being set, particularly in times of fiscal restraint. It is easier to justify cutting a programme in the absence of evidence of its benefit.

As real-time data become more widespread, there is a much greater opportunity to improve analytical turnaround times. Ireland provides an example of where this has added value to quickly provide insight on labour market outcomes following COVID-19, using a real-time lookup of its Revenue Ireland data to analysis labour market outcomes of those using its Pandemic Unemployment Payment (Department of Social Protection, Ireland, 2021[22]).

The United Kingdom offers a comparable example where its use has sped up ALMP evaluation. The design of Universal Credit in the United Kingdom means that real time information on earnings is transferred from Her Majesty's Revenue and Customs to the Department for Work and Pensions (DWP). This allows analysis to be conducted almost in real time, useful both to the operational monitoring of policy but also by reducing lead times on impact evaluations. The randomised control trial on counselling support services to employed individuals run by the DWP demonstrates the value of such real time data exchange. DWP recruited participants between March 2015 and March 2018. In September 2018 it was able to publish its preliminary impact assessment, looking at employment outcomes up to 52 weeks after trial enrolment. By October 2019, it was able to publish an extension to this analysis to 78 weeks (DWP, 2021[23]). In principle, given the real time nature of the data, the minimum amount of time between these two studies could have been just six months. Even so, the turnaround time was rapid for this type of assessment.

The periodicity of the income tax data in Canada also raises questions about its suitability to analyse the impact of EAS, whereby expected programme impacts are relatively short and smaller in scale. The small impact on earnings, of securing a job earlier, is easier to get lost in the noise of annual earnings data. There are also non-trivial questions to answer on the assignment of earnings to pre- and post- treatment periods. For programmes that begin in the middle of the year, it is particularly difficult to know whether annual earnings belong to the treatment or pre-treatment period. ESDC circumvents some of these issues by specifying an "in-programme" year and then looking at years "post-programme". When looking at programmes that might be expected to have longer-term impacts (such as Skills Development) this is unlikely to have substantial impacts on impact assessment. However, for EAS, this could very well mask the shorter-term impact that these services may have on employment, especially as they are often designed with improving jobseekers job search ability and may improve the job matching speed. Other studies looking at these types of programme, that have access to temporally disaggregated data, have demonstrated the impact they have on "in programme year" effects (for example Cheung et al. (2019[24]), DWP (2018[25])).

One of the drivers for ESDC to move to a unified, aggregate assessment was due to the long lead times posed by the bilateral survey-based evaluations. This suggests that timeliness is a dimension to policy making in Canada that has some salience. Therefore, any efforts made to reduce the lead time before data can become available is likely to be a welcome intervention to policy making.

3.4. Quality assurance

Quality assurance of results and exploration of the sensitivity of results to techniques and assumptions within them are critical to ensure accuracy of results, to evaluate risk and to convey the weight of evidence behind the conclusions. ALMP evaluation is complex especially so for programmes which are non-experimental and rely on the creation of a counterfactual group using statistical analysis. ESDC has implemented a range of processes to quality assure the data it uses, the methodologies it employs and the results that it produces, in order to ensure analysis is reliable.

The ESDC teams conducting the impact evaluation follow a series of steps and procedures to quality assure their analysis. The methodology team that sits within the evaluation directorate provides guidelines on the processes to follow in evaluations and separates out the task list into stages. Each of these stages has multiple checks to complete to ensure data accuracy. The four stages are broadly outlined as follows (ESDC, 2021[26]):

- **Evaluation Strategy** – to define strategy for evaluation with ESDC officials and programme teams. Checks are made on the validity and availability of all administrative data and potential outcome variables. The methodology team work with evaluators to check capacity of data to answer research questions and identify outcome indicators.

- **Assessment of Evaluation Strategy** – conducted internally within the project team, to cross-validate the administrative data, perform a literature review and submit data access requests.

- **Data Analysis** – checks with other ESDC branches on data collection and quality assessment. Internal project checks across all data verification (see Box 3.1 for more detail):

- **Final validation** – sharing results and methodology with peer reviewers, compare outcomes with other OECD countries, review against Statistics Canada census data, review code with external contractors.

> ## Box 3.1. ESDC data analysis quality assurance
>
> **Extensive checks are conducted on data to ensure that the data used is reliable and up-to-date**
>
> *Data type* checks are conducted to investigate whether data are of the expected formats in meta data and checks are run to look for missing values or erroneous codes. An assessment of *data quality* is made by tabulating data to ensure its reliability, accuracy, relevance and completeness, following Statistics Canada's data quality guidelines.
>
> *Ranges and frequencies* are checked to ensure values lie within expected ranges (for example, incomes are not negative), and that frequencies remain consistent across the analysis. Any dropped cases are carefully documented with rationale.
>
> *Checks to external totals* are conducted, to ascertain analysis is consistent with other reports (for example the annual ESDC employment insurance Monitoring and Assessment reports).
>
> *Code Check*s are run throughout the code. Syntax and logical errors are checked. Mid-stage datasets are checked against their source files to ensure data has not been lost of inadvertently manipulated.
>
> *Post-Validation Check*s compare results from past evaluations to assess whether observed differences are within expectation or exceed a tolerance threshold.
>
> *Literature reviews* are conducted to take into account recent methodological developments (for example, the move towards using machine learning for sub-group analysis).
>
> *Software check*s are conducted to validate results using different statistical packages (across SAS, Stata, R, and Python).
>
> *Robustness checks* are conducted to validate the net impact results using alternative methods, to determine whether the results change dependent on the method used.
>
> *Sensitivity analysis* is performed which changes key variable assumptions in the work, to determine the extent to which the results are affected by changing parameters.
>
> The range of checks carried out allows ESDC to systematically assess all of the attributes to data quality in their evaluation and how these may impact on its results. Checks on the data used can be especially important with administrative data, particularly where data pertaining to the same individual or programme can be recorded on different systems and provide different answers. Similarly, whilst administrative data are usually high-quality and accurate, it can on occasion be inaccurate. Providing a strong and documented rationale for its inclusion or exclusion in analysis is necessary for transparency and scrutiny. Relationships with wider teams and colleagues can often be helpful in this domain-operational staff can often provide insight to data quality where statistical investigations alone may be insufficient. By having a clear and consistent set of metrics to compare against, it helps to ensure that checks are methodical, repeatable and comprehensive.
>
> Source: ESDC (2021[26]), SSPB ED Quality assurance Methodology (unpublished internal guidance document); Statistics Canada quality guidelines, https://www150.statcan.gc.ca/n1/pub/12-539-x/2019001/ensuring-assurer-eng.htm.

This set of processes is both detailed and comprehensive. As an established set of procedures, it allows the quality assurance process to be recorded and documented. It also allows for an internal discussion of technique validation and checks on data and assumptions, prior to analysis being sent to external peer reviewers. Having this set of procedures in place helps to verify the analysis that has been conducted and ensure it is comprehensive, up-to-date and accurate. This is important because analysis is conducted internally. External quality assurers only advise on the outputs from the analysis and the methodology, they do undertake any detailed scrutiny of data used or the statistical coding that is performed. Having an internal set of processes ensures this work is completed. The methodology team works with the team conducting the evaluation to ensure all the processes are followed. Consultations with expert teams outside of evaluation directorate ensure that the correct expertise is employed to assess the analysis. For example, the data quality team within the Skills and Employment branch, is consulted on the data used in the evaluations, as they have responsibility for the data upload and quality assurance of the LMDA and WDA data and so have expertise on data quality and its suitability for use. Checks across both coding and data allow confidence that analysis is not subject to error which would undermine the reliability of the results. It adheres to the "four eyes principle" in having analysis cross-checked by different individuals. This principle is strengthened further by collaboration with staff in other ESDC units. On issues to do with data processing and extraction, expertise is sought from the Chief Data Officer's team, to ensure that database extraction requests are valid. Results and coding checks are conducted within the evaluation directorate, so that teams that have not directly conducted the work scrutinise the code and the results to corroborate analysis. Once these checks have been completed, results are shared with external peer reviewers who provide expert judgement on them. Additionally contextual checks on the analysis are applied by cross-referencing to known international data and census data from Statistics Canada.

3.5. Increasing data availability

Currently, the availability of data for evaluation of ALMPs sits entirely within ESDC and specifically within the Evaluation Directorate. However, outside of the analysis that ESDC conducts, it is not possible for external researchers to conduct assessments of ALMPs. Improving the availability of data to external researchers could lead to more numerous studies, foster creativity and learning, and cross-validate the existing work produced by ESDC. It is no coincidence that in the meta-analysis by (Card, Kluve and Weber, 2018[27]) the countries that feature with the most evaluations of their policies are the ones with open access to data. Germany, Austria and Switzerland contribute 52 studies. Denmark, Finland, Norway and Sweden contribute 48 studies. But the combined heft of Canada, the United States, the United Kingdom, Australia and New Zealand contribute just 24 (Card, Kluve and Weber, 2018[27]).

3.5.1. Statistics Canada are compiling and making data available for research

Statistics Canada, the national statistics agency, is leading Canada's effort to increase data availability to researchers and does have an option to allow public access to microdata (OECD, 2020[1]). It offers access via two channels:

- Unrestricted access – Public Use Microdata Files (PUMFs) are available to institutions and individuals. They are non-aggregated data, which are carefully modified and then reviewed to ensure that no individual or business is directly or indirectly identified. There are some 145 PUMF available to individuals, either via download individually on the Statistics Canada website or via the use of an institutional subscription service that gives unlimited access to all of the datasets and metadata. Institutions that subscribe also sign a licence agreement.

- Restricted access – Data are available via the use of Research Data Centres, which are secure facilities located in government offices, universities or secure access points in approved locations. Around 150 data files are available for analysis. Researchers are deemed employees of Statistics Canada. Academic users are managed via the Canadian Research Data Centre Network, who provide 33 access points on campuses throughout Canada. For primary university users (including students or employees of the partner universities conducting self-directed research), there are no access fees. Access fees for secondary users vary. For academic researchers of other institutions or government and third sector users, they are CAD 6 250 for the first 200 hours of data access, with fees of CAD 3 250 for additional data access blocks of 100 hours. Private sector users are charged CAD 9 500 for the initial access and CAD 4 750 for 100 additional hours. They are also charged CAD 3 875 per data file requested, whereas academic, government and third sector users pay only CAD 700 per file after an initial allocation of 25 data files.[1]

Despite the drive towards greater open data access, there still exists no comprehensive way to interrogate administrative data on ALMPs, essential to any counterfactual impact assessment of ALMPs. Both the unrestricted and restricted access datasets contain mainly survey data, rather than administrative micro-data. In addition, of the 145 files made available via PUMF, over 100 were released in 2015 or earlier (containing data relating to 2013 and earlier) – limiting the use of datasets for up-to-date policy analysis.

The Research Data Centre data files offer promise for ALMP evaluation but are as yet incomplete for proper evaluation of ALMPs. At present, its repository contains some but not all of the administrative data needed for evaluation:

- Employment insurance Status Vector – 1997-2018: Weekly employment insurance records for claimants, covering the benefits enjoyed by participants and the earnings they report.
- Longitudinal Administrative Databank – 1982-2018: Provides a 20% sample of income tax data from CRA.
- Record of Employment – 1987-2019: Information on job separations, mandatory for employment insurance claimants, containing information on job tenure and other job characteristics related to insurance administration.

No data are available on ALMP participation. There is no facility via the current dataset access to link ALMP data to CRA data in the manner that ESDC uses for its evaluations. Making this a priority would open ESDC policies to the wider research community and would also allow PTs to take a more critical look at their own policy delivery.

3.5.2. Other countries provide examples of how institutions can be used to facilitate data access

Liberalising the use of data access can take different forms but usually revolves around there being a specified government institutes that warehouses register data from different ministries and links these data together. In addition to the examples of *Institut für Arbeitsmarkt* (IAB) in Germany, Stats NZ, Statistics Canada and Statistics the Netherlands (OECD, 2020[1]), there are several countries with innovative and extensive data collections for external researchers, organised around different access and warehousing protocols.

Some countries utilise statistics institutes to collate data and securely share it. Similar to Canada, Statistics Finland, the public institution with responsibility for statistics and data in Finland, collates, organises and links high-quality register data. It houses almost 160 sources of data which include ALMPs, income and tax, education, socio-economic status including detailed family status, occupation, health and education data, making it one of the most comprehensive sources of high-quality administrative data available. Researchers can apply for data and make use of its FIONA system to access the data securely via remote means. Bespoke datasets can also be created for researchers upon request, subject to extra charges and longer lead times. Users can also request that their own datasets be uploaded to the secure environment, so that they may make use of these in analysis.

The Federal Statistical Office (BFS) of Switzerland provides access to anonymised individual register data and provides data linking services between registers. As of 2016, BFS had 56 linkage agreements for statistical and longitudinal analysis with research institutions, federal and cantonal authorities and other organisations.

Stats NZ offers a range of linked administrative data using its Integrated Data Infrastructure and Longitudinal Business Dataset. Like Statistics Canada, researchers can use data in approved facilities.

Costs for access and use of the datasets are low. There is an assessment fee of NZD 500 (waived for government and unsuccessful applications) and a fee of NZD 155 per hour for confidentiality checking of results (free for the first 15 hours) (Stats NZ, 2021[28]). Storage of data up to 200 GB is free and NZD 1.50 per GB per month after that. There is a six-week cycle of application approvals, ensuring a quick turnaround to applications. As of November 2019, Stats NZ had over 600 researchers using its data, comprising over 250 projects. This has resulted in 116 evaluations of separate interventions on ALMPs (de Boer, 2019[29]).

Quasi-governmental autonomous bodies are used in other countries for making data accessible to researchers. Sweden's Institute for Labour Market Policy Evaluation (IFAU) is a state-owned research institute. It does not make any proposals or recommendations in its own reports. Its objective is to promote, support and carry out scientific evaluations on the labour market but this includes influencing the collection of data and making data easily available to researchers, both in Sweden and abroad.

France has sought to establish better public-private links with its external data centre. Its *Centre d'Accès Sécurisé aux Données* (CASD) is a public interest group bringing together public and private sector researchers, the State represented by INSEE, GENES, CNRS, École Polytechnique and HEC Paris and was created by ministerial decree in December 2018. Its main purpose is "to organise and implement secure access services for confidential data for non-profit research, study, evaluation or innovation, activities described as "research services", mainly public. Its mission is also to promote the technology developed to secure access to data in the private sector".[2] Data are available from INSEE, the Ministries of Justice, National Education, Agriculture and Food, Economy and Finance. It has 400 data sources, over 3 000 users and has amassed some 400 publications and communications since its inception only three years ago.

3.6. Summary

The creation of a comprehensive data platform for analysis and the incorporation of CRA data into it has paved the way for ESDC to conduct high quality impact analysis of its ALMPs. This platform provides efficiency and stability as a basis for impact evaluations. Detailed information on participants' characteristics and their outcomes in the labour market allows impacts of programmes to be thoroughly assessed. Information on past earnings and benefit receipt, alongside broader socio-economic data, means that careful comparison is possible between participants and non-participants in ALMPs. ESDC makes a clever change to the comparison group for former employment insurance claimants, to ensure it is possible to construct a plausible counterfactual where the administrative data alone may not be sufficient. Individuals are disaggregated into sub-groups, which allows for a richer policy narrative to be developed on the impacts of ALMPs.

However there is still room for improvement to the data used that would permit even more colour to be given to policy assessment. Information on job type and tenure would allow more discussion of job quality. Income data that are more temporally disaggregated would allow better discussion of job counselling services. Better data on families and education would permit a more complete assessment of the impacts of ALMPs on parents and young people. Lags to the collection of income data also mean there is a constraint on feasible analytical timelines.

Availability of the data to conduct research is currently confined to internal ESDC analysts. Small changes to the availability of data via Statistics Canada would permit external researchers to conduct such research. This would allow ESDC to benefit from greater democratisation of its programme evaluation work, permitting greater innovation and cross-referencing of analysis, such as is already happening in countries which have made greater strides in this area.

References

Aho, S. et al. (2018), *Työvoimapalvelujen kohdistuminen ja niihin osallistuvien työllistyminen*, https://julkaisut.valtioneuvosto.fi/bitstream/handle/10024/160639/19-2018-Tyovoimapalvelujen%20kohdistuminenpdf.pdf. [16]

Algan, Crépon and Glover (2020), "Are Active Labor Market Policies Directed at Firms Effective? Evidence from a Randomized Evaluation with Local Employment Agencies", https://www.povertyactionlab.org/sites/default/files/research-paper/5484_Active-Labor-Markets-Evidence-from-Public-Service-France_January2020.pdf. [21]

Andersson, F. et al. (2013), "Does Federally-Funded Job Training Work? Nonexperimental Estimates of WIA Training Impacts Using Longitudinal Data on Workers and Firms", *NBER working paper series*, http://www.nber.org/papers/w19446. [19]

Arni, P., R. Lalive and J. Van Ours (2012), "How effective are unemployment benefit sanctions? Looking beyond unemployment exit", *Journal of Applied Econometrics*, Vol. 28/7, pp. 1153–1178, https://doi.org/10.1002/jae.2289. [20]

Bellemare, C., N. Kyui and G. Lacroix (2021), "Immigrants' Economic Performance and Selective Outmigration: Diverging Predictions from Survey and Administrative Data", *SSRN Electronic Journal*, https://doi.org/10.2139/ssrn.3811772. [18]

Card, D., J. Kluve and A. Weber (2018), "What Works? A Meta Analysis of Recent Active Labor Market Program Evaluations", *Journal of the European Economic Association*, Vol. 16/3, pp. 894-931, https://doi.org/10.1093/JEEA/JVX028. [27]

Cheung, M. et al. (2019), "Does Job Search Assistance Reduce Unemployment? Experimental Evidence on Displacement Effects and Mechanisms", *SSRN Electronic Journal*, https://doi.org/10.2139/SSRN.3515935. [24]

de Boer and Ku (2018), *Cost-effectiveness of MSD employment assistance*, Ministry of Social Development, New Zealand, https://www.msd.govt.nz/documents/about-msd-and-our-work/publications-resources/research/employment-assistance-effectiveness/ea-effectiveness-report-07022019.pdf. [12]

de Boer and Ku (2018), *Effectiveness of the Limited Service Volunteer programme in 2014/15*, Ministry of Social Development, New Zealand, https://www.msd.govt.nz/documents/about-msd-and-our-work/publications-resources/evaluation/lsv-effectiveness/lsv-effectiveness.pdf. [13]

de Boer, M. (2019), *Monitoring ALMP effectiveness using linked data: The New Zealand experience*, https://www.oecd.org/employment/emp/S3.3.%20De%20Boer_NZL.pdf. [29]

Department of Social Protection, Ireland (2021), *Working Paper: Employment Transitions of People Closing PUP Claims*, https://assets.gov.ie/203173/a9f36c82-e218-464f-a464-897932ff8931.pdf. [22]

DWP (2021), *Work and Health Progamme statistics: background information and methodology*, Department for Work & Pensions, United Kingdom, https://www.gov.uk/government/publications/work-and-health-programme-statistics-background-information-and-methodology/work-and-health-progamme-statistics-background-information-and-methodology (accessed on 20 December 2021). [23]

DWP (2018), *Weekly work search review trial*, Department for Work & Pensions, United Kingdom, https://www.gov.uk/government/publications/jobseekers-allowance-weekly-work-search-review-trial (accessed on 26 November 2021).
[25]

ESDC (2021), *Analysis of Employment Benefits and Support Measures (EBSM) Profile and Medium-Term Incremental Impacts from 2010 to 2017*, Employment and Social Development Canada (unpublished).
[10]

ESDC (2021), *Labour Market Program Data Platform - Data Dictionary v3.05a*, Employment and Social Development Canada (unpublished).
[4]

ESDC (2021), *SSPB ED Quality assurance Methodology*, Employment and Social Development Canada (unpublished).
[26]

ESDC (2020), *Horizontal Evaluation of the Youth Employment Strategy: Skills Link Stream*, Employment and Social Development Canada, https://www.canada.ca/en/employment-social-development/corporate/reports/evaluations/horizontal-skills-link.html.
[3]

ESDC (2019), *Quantitative Methodology Report – Final*, Employment and Social Development Canada (unpublished).
[9]

ESDC (2017), *Evaluation of the Labour Market Development Agreements: Synthesis Report*, Employment and Social Development Canada, https://publications.gc.ca/site/eng/9.841271/publication.html.
[8]

Gingras, Y. et al. (2017), "Making Evaluation More Responsive to Policy Needs: The Case of the Labour Market Development Agreements", *Canadian Journal of Program Evaluation*, Vol. 32/2, https://doi.org/10.3138/cjpe.31119.
[2]

Handouyahia, A. (2019), *The creation of a rich data platform to support net impact evaluation of Labour Market Programmes*, https://www.oecd.org/employment/emp/S4.5.%20Handouyahia_CAN.pdf.
[5]

Heckman, J., R. Lalonde and J. Smith (1999), "The Economics and Econometrics of Active Labor Market Programs", in *Handbook of Labor Economics*, Elsevier, https://doi.org/10.1016/s1573-4463(99)03012-6.
[6]

Lechner, M. and C. Wunsch (2013), "Sensitivity of matching-based program evaluations to the availability of control variables", *Labour Economics*, Vol. 21, pp. 111-121, https://doi.org/10.1016/J.LABECO.2013.01.004.
[7]

Meyer, B., W. Mok and J. Sullivan (2015), "Household Surveys in Crisis", *Journal of Economic Perspectives*, Vol. 29/4, pp. 199-226, https://doi.org/10.1257/jep.29.4.199.
[17]

OECD (2021), *OECD Employment Outlook 2021*, OECD Publishing, Paris, https://doi.org/10.1787/5a700c4b-en.
[14]

OECD (2020), "Impact evaluation of labour market policies through the use of linked administrative data", OECD, Paris, https://www.oecd.org/els/emp/Impact_evaluation_of_LMP.pdf.
[1]

Statistics Canada (2021), *Time spent on unpaid care of a child in the household, by working arrangement and age of youngest child, Canada, 2010*, https://www150.statcan.gc.ca/n1/pub/89-503-x/2010001/article/11546/tbl/tbl006-eng.htm.
[11]

Statistics Finland (2022), *Research Data Catalogue*, https://taika.stat.fi/. [15]

Stats NZ (2021), *Apply to use microdata for research*, https://www.stats.govt.nz/integrated-data/apply-to-use-microdata-for-research/. [28]

Notes

[1] https://www.statcan.gc.ca/en/microdata/data-centres/fees.

[2] https://www.casd.eu/en/le-centre-dacces-securise-aux-donnees-casd/gouvernance-et-missions/.

4 Assessing the impact: methodologies, evaluation and cost benefit analysis

Accurate policy assessment requires rigorous analytical techniques. Employment and Social Development Canada (ESDC) uses an observational study, relying on a rich set of administrative data to compare participants in active labour market policies and non-participants. ESDC extends this analysis further to conduct cost-benefit assessment which allows programmes with different underlying costs to be compared against one another and to look at value-for-money. ESDC delivers all of this analysis using a well-resourced internal evaluation function, meaning it retains flexibility in its delivery and has continued expertise in the methodology and data used. This is supplemented with external expert peer reviews, which provides guidance on the methods used and the outputs produced.

4.1. Introduction

The problem at the heart of any policy evaluation is to accurately calculate the impact of the policy on an individual's outcomes. Attributing observed changes to the policy requires isolating the particular contribution of the intervention and ensuring that causality runs from the intervention to the outcome (Leeuw and Vaessen, 2009[1]). For an individual that participates in a programme, what would have happened to them had they not participated is never observed. The construction of this "counterfactual" is crucial to being able to estimate the programme's effect. It relies on estimation of the programme impact, absent any differences that may occur from the comparison of individuals that would otherwise experience different outcomes. Employment and Social Development Canada (ESDC) approach these issues in a methodical and rigorous manner, employing robust analytical techniques to construct groups of non-participants to use as a counterfactual and identify the impact of active labour market policies (ALMPs). Crucially, they also extend this analysis to incorporate programme costs and analyse value for money, which is essential to properly compare policies to one another.

4.2. Types of evaluation design

There is a considerable literature on the various empirical techniques that can be employed to address "selection bias" (see DiNardo and Lee (2011[2]) for a discussion), that individuals participating in a particular programme might be materially different to those that do not. A simple taxonomy is utilised below that provides insight into the different strategies that an evaluator can employ to recover the causal effect of a programme (OECD, 2020[3]). This serves as a useful framework to contextualise how ESDC conducts its counterfactual impact CIE and what the alternatives to them are. It is split by (i) whether the evaluator can control participation in the intervention (experimental vs. observational studies) and (ii) within each of these two categories, the specific research design (or "methods").

Observational studies can be classified into two types of research design – with the key difference between them being whether the respective method assumes selection only on observable characteristics or also on unobservable characteristics (Table 4.1). Observable characteristics are the known attributes of an individual (for example, age, gender, place of residence), whereas unobservable characteristics refer to everything else that may influence actions (for example, motivation or ability) but for which no data are available. The research designs differ in their approach to constructing a credible comparison group (DiNardo and Lee, 2011[2]; Heckman, Lalonde and Smith, 1999[4]; Kluve and Stöterau, 2014[5]; Wooldridge, 2009[6]). Data needs differ significantly on the type of analytical method chosen. Methods assuming selection on observables require rich contextual data to compare alike people. Observable characteristics in ESDC's analysis include all of those listed in Chapter 3, Table 3.2. Methods assuming selection on unobservables as well do not require such rich data, but instead rely on a different construction of the counterfactual group using assumptions that mean comparisons can be made as if they were random.

Countries use a mix of identification strategies to evaluate policy. In the data included in the Card, Kluve and Weber (2018[7]) meta-analysis, of the 174 studies included from OECD countries, 104 (60%) used selection on observables, 40 (23%) used exogenous variation (selection on unobservables and observables) and 30 (17%) used random assignment.[1] The precise mixture used in a particular country will be the result of technical, practical, ethical and political decisions on the feasibility of the different methods used, but the significant minority of countries that undertook randomised studies comprise is notable.

Table 4.1. Types of impact evaluation designs

Experimental studies	Observational studies	
	Selection on observables and unobservables	Selection on observables
Randomised assignment (incl. over-subscription)	Instrumental Variables (IV)	Covariate adjustment
Conditional randomised assignment / (raised) threshold randomisation	Regression discontinuity design (RDD)	Statistical matching
Randomised phase-in	Difference-in-Difference (DID)	
Randomised encouragement		

Source: OECD (2020[3]), "Impact Evaluations Framework for the Spanish Ministry of Labour and Social Economy and Ministry of Inclusion, Social Security and Migrations", http://t4.oecd.org/els/emp/Impact_Evaluations_Framework.pdf, adapted based on Kluve and Stöterau (2014[5]), "A Systematic Framework for Measuring Employment Impacts of Development Co-operation Interventions", https://energypedia.info/images/5/54/A_Systematic_Framework_for_Measuring_Employment_Impacts_of_Development_Cooperation_Interventions.pdf.

Some countries (for example Canada and Finland) currently employ only observational studies to derive estimates of programme impacts. This allows them to deliver policy without having to devote extra resources to planning evaluation and trial design, but means that they have to make stronger assumptions about their analysis to have confidence in the estimates produced. Many countries (for example France, Germany, Korea and the United Kingdom) use some mix of randomised studies and observational studies to evaluate different policies. Countries such as Denmark and Switzerland, that have localised delivery of ALMPs similar to that in Canada, work with their localities to employ randomised studies and generate evidence on policy effectiveness. The extent to which a country uses one or the other depends on the factors mentioned above and the specific research questions to hand. The benefit of using observational studies of programmes that have already been implemented is that is it always possible, subject to the right data being available, to analyse a programme, including during its operation or after its completion.

4.2.1. ESDC uses rigorous methods based on observational studies to conduct impact assessment

ESDC uses an observational methodology to evaluate ALMPs – it looks at individuals who participated in ALMPs and evaluates the impact of the programme on their subsequent outcomes. A combination of statistical matching and difference-in-difference (DID) analysis is used by ESDC to conduct impact evaluation of the LMDA. Both are examples of observational studies (Table 4.1), but they are used in conjunction with one another. In the third cycle of LMDA evaluation, the broad steps to ESDC's analytical methodology are:

1. Preparatory matching (using Coarsened Exact Matching, CEM) – this step conducted in the data exploration stage to find a better comparison pool, so that it speeds up both computation times and analytical resource requirements

2. Matching (using Propensity Score Matching) – to construct comparison groups of participants and non-participants

3. Outcome assessment – using difference-in-difference methodology to estimate final programme impacts

Both of the first two steps are examples of matching, utilising the methodology outlined in Box 4.1, but they are used in sequence by ESDC to expedite analysis. Step 1 was introduced as part of the third cycle of evaluation for two primary purposes; to improve computation times and reduce analytical re-working in Step 2 (ESDC, 2019[8]).

The properties of CEM are such that it is easy to implement, tractable, and may result in better variable balance relative to matching techniques used in step two (Iacus, King and Porro, 2012[9]). Balance is the degree to which a variable in the participant group has the same distribution of values as that in the non-participant group (this is usually assessed looking at the mean values for the groups- for example, using age, whether they contain individuals with the same average age). The process involves the user specifying levels of "coarseness" of data. In an analysis of age, rather than taking an exact age, specifying categories – for instance 30 and under, and over 30. The "exact" nature of the matching means that any data point without a match is removed from the process. In an example dataset with two individuals, a participant aged 30 and a non-participant aged 31, no match would be possible using the previous thresholds. If the participant was aged 60 however, a match would be made (because both the participant and non-participant are aged 30 or over, the threshold chosen). This exemplifies two features of the process, firstly that the analyst has control over the definition of the categories into which the variables describing participants and non-participants are being classified (their level of "coarseness"), and secondly that the choice of categories has a critical impact on being able to find matches. In addition, as the number of observable variables used increases, it becomes harder to find matching samples with the same unique characteristics. This increases the number of participant cases dropped from the sample.

In step two, propensity score matching (PSM) is then applied to the participants and non-participants left in the sample. Using the observable characteristics for both sets of individuals, the likelihood of participating in the programme is estimated, with the observable characteristics influencing the likelihood of that participation. This score is a probability between 0 and 1, with probabilities closer to 1 meaning an individual is more likely to participate. This probability acts as an "index of similarity" between participants and non-participants. Participants are matched to programme-eligible non-participants on this score. For example, a non-participant with a propensity score of 0.8 is more likely to be matched a participant with a propensity score of 0.7 than they are with a participant with a score of 0.3. It matches non-participants that look like they should have participated but didn't, to similar participants who look like they should have participated and did (and vice-versa for the individuals that look like they should not participate). In the example using only age, if being young gave a higher likelihood of participation in a programme, it would match young participants to young non-participants. In this sense, it is intuitive to see how matching starts to "balance" the participant and non-participant group along the observable dimensions that determine participation. When the number of variables increases, this balancing can be difficult to achieve – an iteration of matching can increase the balance of one variable but at the expense of causing the deterioration of balance in another variable. This can leave the analyst in a situation of having to repeatedly "tweak" the analysis in an attempt to improve the balance. This is the situation that ESDC have tried to mitigate by implementing the step one CEM. After this process has been completed, the participant and non-participant groups that are matched to one another should be similar in all the observable characteristics used. Any differences remaining between the outcomes of the individuals should be as the result of the participants having completed the programme. Similar to CEM, it is possible to estimate programme effects using the groups defined by this analysis.

In step three, ESDC proceed to make their final estimation of programme impacts, using a DID methodology. There is no additional need to process on the characteristics of individuals, as this estimation explicitly assumes selection on unobservables (as well as observable characteristics) – all differences between individuals are accounted for. The participant and non-participants groups have already been chosen in the preceding steps. The important assumption made that DID makes is that the differences between participants and non-participants remain fixed over time. It does this by looking at how income changes before and after the programme for participants and non-participants (see Box 4.1). Because PSM can only control for characteristics that are observable, this step provides an extra layer of assurance. For example, if education determines participation in a programme and also influences earnings but is not directly observed, DID can control for its impact whereas PSM would not.

The question might be asked, if DID can control for all differences between individuals, whether observed or unobserved, then what is the rationale for using matching prior to it? Part of this is related to the DID assumption that differences between participants and non-participants are fixed over time. Going back to the example using age, if participants in a programme were younger and non-participants older and if young people tend to "catch up" to their older counterparts' earnings as they become older, then we might expect to see the pre-programme difference in earnings between the groups changing over time. This would introduce bias into the DID estimate. Using matching to control for these time-varying trends can improve the accuracy of the DID estimate.

The combination of techniques helps to strengthen analysis

The use of both matching and DID serves as a strong foundation for impact assessment. The problem for analysis using observational studies is that they rely on the assumption that participants and non-participants are comparable after the analysis has been completed, which is often never fully testable. In the case of those techniques using selection on observables (including matching), it is the assumption that all the data you have information on explain the entire difference between individuals and there is nothing in addition. Whilst utilising pre-programme outcomes (such as income and benefit receipt) in the propensity score, to ensure participants and non-participants are statistically equivalent, provides a strong argument that groups are comparable it cannot be proven. For DID then is an assumption that differences are stable over time. This stability is only testable in the pre-participation period, not after participation. By combining matching and DID it helps to address some of the potential shortcomings that having observational data bring to inference, by combining their strong points. Both of these techniques are commonplace in the wider literature on ALMPs and so their use as a methodology for inference is well documented and understood. In this sense, ESDC has set a very good platform on which to base its evaluation.

The use of CEM in the first step is an interesting one that is worth considering further. A recent paper on Lithuania uses a similar methodology when evaluating training subsidies (OECD, 2022[10]). Because the programme is designed for individuals outside of "prime age", meaning younger and older individuals are selected, programme participants have an unusual age distribution. This created problems when using PSM to compare participants and non-participants. It was not possible to match (or "balance") the age distributions because of this. By first pre-processing with CEM, using age as the matching variable, the problems of balancing in PSM were resolved. Canada implements CEM for similar but slightly different reasons – to reduce the pool of non-participants and speed up the computation times (which can be considerable given the large numbers of participants and variables for analysis) and to help expedite the balancing required when using PSM. It does not do the latter for explicit reasons to do with a particular policy rule that causes certain people to participate, but rather to mitigate general analytical complexity that uses a lot of analytical resource. These examples suggest that CEM can offer practical solutions to some of the issues encountered with counterfactual impact analysis using PSM.

Explicit comparison of the separate stages could provide greater insight

ESDC could consider further discussion on the combination of methodologies it employs to add further insight to the analysis. Because it conducts two types of assessment, PSM and DID, there is a possibility to separate the steps in this analysis to add additional explanatory power to it. They already include charts of pre-programme earnings before and after matching (ESDC, 2019[8]). By further enriching the discussion around these and the implications for the DID analysis, they could provide greater context on how the estimates change between groups, using the methods chosen, and what the reasons underlying any change might be. Large changes between the PSM estimate and the estimate with DID layered on top would suggest the latter is controlling for unobservable characteristics that the former could not. This could then give rise to discussion of whether those unobservable characteristics might plausibly be time-varying, and how much confidence could be placed on these estimates. There is no simple black-and-white best practice in these assessments, because of the degree of judgement and uncertainty involved, but even having this information for the different programmes that comprise the LMDA may allow for a more involved discussion on the relative effects, and confidence in the underlying estimates. Having more discussion around this, even if only contained with a technical annex, would provide more information on the performance of the estimators and further assurance of the process.

Box 4.1. An illustration of the techniques used by ESDC in their impact evaluation

Figure 4.1. A comparison of random assignment, matching and difference-in-difference

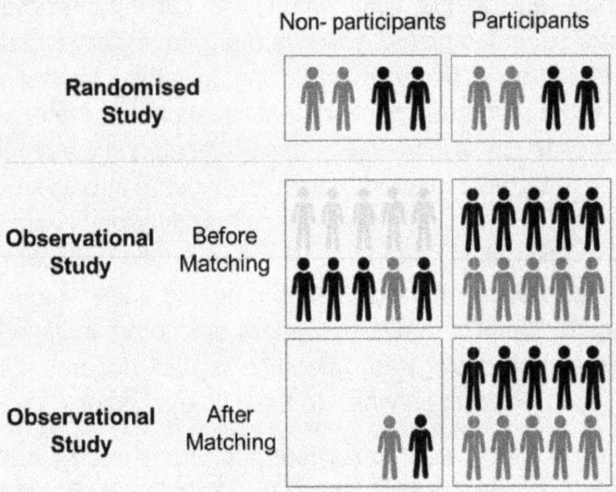

		Difference-in-Difference	
		Non- participant	Participant
Income before programme		$3	$2
Income after programme		$10	$12
Difference in Income		$7	$10
Difference-in-Difference			$3

In a **randomised study**, the fact that the participants are randomly selected ensures that those who do and not do participate are alike (statistically equivalent). There are no underlying reasons driving differences between the two sets of individual. In this instance, programme effects can be estimated by comparing the outcomes of participants against non-participants. No other data are required.

Observational studies occur when a programme is already implemented and random selection is no longer possible. For these programmes, there is a possibility for participants and non-participants to be different because individuals that opt-in to the programme are different to those that do not. For example, a computer training course might attract younger people. If being young is also related to earnings after the programme, then a simple comparison of participants (young people) against non-participants (old people) would lead to an incorrect estimate of the programme's effect. To see the effects of unobserved characteristics, consider "motivation". Suppose having higher intrinsic "motivation" led to higher earnings but also increased the likelihood of participation in a training course. If this motivation was unobservable and it was not possible to discern which participants and non-participants were more/less motivated, programmes effect would be overestimated. A conclusion would lead to the training course having beneficial effects on earnings, when actually it just contained a group of participants who would have earnt more even in the absence of the programme. However, if this motivation was also linked to past earnings, and data were available on past earnings, these earnings data could remove some of this phenomenon indirectly (as motivation is highly likely to be reflected in the level of earnings). The degree to which they were able to do that, would depend on the strength of association between motivation and past earnings.

Matching aims to only compare non-participants that are similar to participants. Matching is achieved by comparing participants and programme-eligible non-participants on variables that affect decisions to enter the programme (e.g. age). There are various different methods of matching, but they utilise the same underlying principle and differ only in how they choose the match between people. This can include allowing one individual to match to many, if they are the closest match to all of their pairs, or by removing the individual once they have matched their closest partner. An efficient way to measure the similarity between individuals is to collapse all critical variables affecting programme selection into a single index, such as a propensity-score.

By contrast, **difference-in-difference,** does not use observed characteristics of individuals at all, but looks at the change in outcome for participants after the programme, relative to before the programme, compared to the change in outcome over the same period for non-participants. The difference between these two amounts is the impact of the programme. In this way it automatically accounts for all differences for individuals, because it only looks at relative changes between the two groups. This is dependent on those differences between groups remaining stable over time.

Participants are split by their employment insurance eligibility

As discussed in Chapter 3, participants are partitioned according to their status for Employment Insurance. This is done because of concerns about constructing a valid non-participant comparison group for the former Employment Insurance claimants. This is primarily due to having insufficient administrative data to be able to fully identify the pool of eligible non-participants, because non-participants must also be full-time unemployed, anticipating job loss or have been forced to leave a job due to health reasons, which is not information held by ESDC (ESDC, 2019[8]). ESDC are also concerned that motivation plays a big part in their decision to participate in ALMPs. Motivation is not something "observed", there are no administrative data on it. It may not also be stable over time- for example, a life event related to a death or a change in relationship status, could motivate someone to re-enter the labour market and participate in an ALMP, but would not be observable unless information was obtained on those events. Therefore differences in participants and non-participants may change over time. For these reasons, ESDC decided to change their comparison group, so they compared participants to non-participants of the ALMP in question, but who did participate in Employment Assistance Services (Table 4.2), one of their less intensive ALMPs. Whilst this changes the interpretation of the estimate, compared to the estimate for the current employment insurance claimants, it serves to better mitigate any potential effects of motivation because it compares against people who have already come forward for other services.

A useful lesson to draw from this particular step in ESDC's analysis, is that is important to think carefully about participant and non-participant groups prior to any impact analysis, to carefully dissect reasons on why they may be different and how these differences may manifest themselves over time. In this way careful consideration can be given to the assumptions underlying any impact assessment and how these may be addressed in the analysis.

Table 4.2. ESDC split the impact analysis into two groups based on how they define their comparison group

ALMP Participant Group	Comparison Group
Current employment insurance Claimants	Current employment insurance Claimants with no ALMP Participation
Former employment insurance Claimants	Former employment insurance Claimants only participating in Employment Assistance Services

Source: ESDC (2019[8]), "Quantitative Methodology Report – Final".

4.2.2. Experiments could be used to build additional knowledge in a robust and structured manner

In analytical terms, an experimental study is usually seen as "gold standard" because the process of randomisation ensures that no selection effects exist (see Box 4.1). Participation in a programme is statistically independent of outcomes. Participants and non-participants are alike in every observable and non-observable way, therefore estimated programme effects are unbiased by definition. Experiments also allow policy and delivery ideas to be tested on a smaller scale, to ensure they are effective and offer value-for-money, before they are rolled out further.

This intuitive appeal of randomised studies can often be outweighed by practical issues to their implementation. They involve denial of service to some individuals, which can engender different issues. If there is a political or social imperative to roll policies out immediately, it may not be possible to restrict service in this manner. Localised trials may not also generalise well to the broader population. Furthermore, there can be ethical issues around denial of service to some individuals. These can be compounded in the legal framework of countries, which may explicitly preclude such matters. Due to these issues, relatively few countries, overwhelmingly use randomised studies to evaluate policy. However, they can be useful additions to policy analysis, particularly when they are designed proactively, so as to test areas of interest for policy makers, where existing evidence may be scant.

Denmark and Switzerland offer examples evidence building using randomised trials with locally delivered ALMPs

Denmark is notable for its strategy of employing randomised studies on a systematic and sustained basis to inform policies (see Box 4.2 for more details on Denmark's approach). Its gradual and systematic building of evidence using RCTs contrasts to the Canadian approach, where incremental impacts are repeated regularly on a cyclical basis. This has meant that the same programmes are evaluated in the same manner, albeit for updated time periods. Relationships between officials at the Danish Agency for Labour Market and Recruitment (STAR) and in municipalities are important, because although the planning for the trials is done centrally, they are conducted at the municipal level and rest on agreement to participate from the municipalities themselves. Funding is attached to these experiments to incentivise participation and cover costs. The nature of volunteering by municipalities does introduce some challenges for STAR, who would ideally like to have a mixture of big and small municipalities, so that the individuals participating are representative of the characteristics of the broader population and of labour market opportunities of Denmark as a whole. This cannot be guaranteed and so the relationships between central and municipal colleagues becomes essential to foster collaboration and encourage participation. Similar good relationships have already been built by ESDC with PTs colleagues over the years of the joint evaluation work on the LMDA, which could provide a fruitful ground for any future work in this area.

Box 4.2. Denmark has an evidence strategy strongly grounded in experiments

The Ministry of Employment's evidence strategy is based around the continuous development and implementation of policy and legislation. This can be viewed as a cyclical process comprising of policy proposals; agreement on legislation; implementation of legislation; and finally the evaluation of legislation. In every step evidence-based knowledge plays a crucial role to aid decision-making.

Pursuing an analytical strategy using RCTs has allowed Denmark to systematically address different policy choices and target groups in its ALMPs in a sequential manner. It started by addressing the adequacy of interviews and early interventions on its core client groups, before proceeding to look at more marginalised groups and evaluating differences in delivery strategies. It has now focussed its analytical resources at the hardest to help groups and on using more nuanced methods of ALMP support based around conversation and psychological support.

Proceeding with a rigorous strategy, based on randomised studies where possible, has allowed Denmark to progressively build evidence and enrich its understanding of how ALMPs work in the Danish context. Utilisation of randomised trials means that programmes can be run at a smaller scale and can be focussed on specific policy or delivery objectives.

Table 4.3. RCTS have progressively built knowledge

Name of Trial	Year	Description of Trial
Individual Placement and Support	Ongoing	An evidence-based approach to supported employment for people who have a severe mental illness
Sherpa	Ongoing	Through the use of Sherpa mentors, job consultancy guides and company-based training, this intervention helps people with less severe mental illnesses into work.
Lær at tackle job og sygdom	Ongoing	A course for people suffering from illness who are in receipt of sickness benefits, with a focus on how to deal with illness and focus on job opportunities.
Den gode samtale 2	Ongoing	A nudge experiment on using conversation
Jobfirst	Ongoing	A systematic company-based intervention for vulnerable recipients of benefits.
IBBIS	Ongoing	An intervention testing whether the integration of employment and health care efforts for long-term sick-listed with mental health problems can improve employment outcomes.
LVU-forsøget	2011-12	Job centre intervention versus intervention by private agencies – unemployed persons in long-term education/academics
På rette vej i job	2010-12	Caseworker interviews, company-based training, company based mentoring – recipients of social benefits
Unge-Godt i gang	2009-10	Caseworker interviews, early activations, mentors – young people under the age of 30 with and without education)
Aktive Hurtigere tilbage	2009	Caseworker interviews, activation of recipients of sickness benefits
Hurtigt i gang 2	2008-09	Early and intensive intervention, caseworker interviews and early activation. Different design from Hurtigt i gang 1
Alle i gang	2008	Caseworker interviews, long-term recipients of social benefits
Hurtigt i gang 1	2005-06	Early and intensive intervention, caseworker interviews and early activation, new UIB

Source: The Danish Agency for Labour Market and Recruitment (STAR) (2019[11]), https://www.star.dk/en/evidence-based-policy-making/, Rosholm and Svarer (2009[12]), "Kvantitativ evaluering af Hurtig i gang 2 Af"; Krogh Graversen, Damgaard and Rosdahl (2007[13]), "Hurtigt I Gang"; Rosholm and Svarer (2009[14]), "Kvantitativ evaluering af Alle i Gang"; Svarer et al. (2014[15]), "Evaluering af mentorindsats til unge uden uddannel- se og job"; Boll and Hertz (2009[16]), "Aktive Hurtigere tilbarge"; Boll et al. (2013[17]), "Evaluering På rette vej – i job"; Høeberg et al. (2011[18]), "Evaluering Unge-Godt i gang".

Switzerland also provides a useful example in the incorporation of RCTs to build evidence, in a largely decentralised structure. This evolution has perhaps proceeded in a more organic fashion, building from localised trials before coalescing at a federal level. Switzerland's first RCT in the labour market conducted in the Canton of Aargau and looked at avoiding long-term unemployment of older jobseekers (Arni, 2011[19]). The successful delivery of this RCT, which demonstrated the feasibility and use of such experiments in the Swiss context, then paved the way for incorporation of two further trials. The Supervisory Committee for the Compensation Fund of Unemployment Insurance organises its evidence building research programmes into waves, including the possibility of collaboration with external researchers. As part of its third wave of evaluation of ALMPs for the Supervisory Committee two new trials were included, evaluating the role of social networks and expectations in job and counselling (Arni et al., 2013[20]; Arni and Schiprowski, 2015[21]). This work has culminated in a larger-scale programme of work, directly tendered for through the State Secretariat for Economic Affairs, with two trials to assess the quality and intensity of job counselling services provided in Switzerland (SECO, 2021[22]).

By taking an approach that is more localised in nature, using trials in some PTs, Canada can further proactively build its evidence base, focussing the evidence gathering on mutually agreed evidence gaps and enriching what is known about ALMP delivery, particularly trying to understand specific mechanisms of different programmes and how they deliver outcomes for participants.

4.3. Checks on analysis robustness and uncertainty

The discussion in the previous section highlighted some of the uncertainties that are present when using observational studies for policy evaluation. There are a number of procedures and best practices that should be employed in order to check that the data and methods conform to expectations and produce robust and reliable results. ESDC is comprehensive and methodical in its application of these checks to its analysis in order to determine that its results are reliable and it works through these systematically.

4.3.1. Specification checks are used to assess suitability of statistical models

In order to conduct the PSM that ESDC use to define their participant and non-participant groups, the likelihood of an individual participating in the programme has to be estimated (their "propensity score"). This technique relies upon using the individual's characteristics to determine what impact they have on this likelihood. ESDC conducts specification checks, to evaluate whether the variables chosen to construct this estimate have stability (do not vary significantly when incorporating other variables) and can accurately predict this probability.

For example, if age was the only variable used to construct the propensity score and it gave a 30-year-old individual a propensity score of 0.3 of entering the programme, but when the fact that they had no secondary level education was added to the estimation it changed this score to 0.8, the model on age alone would be mis-specified. This is because another variable (education in this case) affected the likelihood of participation but was omitted from the first estimation. This can happen if variables that are important are left out, but it can also happen if too many variables are included in the estimation. In this case the model is said to be "over-fitted". Instead of picking up true relationships in the data, the model specification too closely mimics the data it is built on. In this instance, estimates can become quite unstable, and adding or removing an additional variable can cause estimates to move dramatically. ESDC also conducts thorough checks of whether different algorithms used to match on the propensity score influence results, using four different algorithms to compare results.

Testing is done to ascertain what variables should be included and how much the results change with different combinations of variables

ESDC uses a statistical technique to determine which variables from their administrative data should be included into the estimation model.[2] This step helps to ensure that the variables chosen are important to the estimation of the propensity score. In cycle three of their evaluation work, this step dropped three variables from their original dataset (ESDC, 2021[23]). However, additional testing was implemented by estimating a model including those three variables into the propensity score estimation, which did not change the results markedly. This gives additional reassurance on the model specification. Statistical tests rely in some way on a comparison to thresholds to determine whether or not a test is passed and these thresholds are often chosen by the researcher. Proceeding in this manner and re-checking the full model, notwithstanding the original test results, is a useful additional practical step that ESDC takes to check analysis and the sensitivity of results.

ESDC compute an estimate for the LMDAs for Canada, but then they also derive separate estimates for each of the 12 PTs. By doing this, they are estimating separate models for each of the PTs. This means the models are specified differently. For example, whilst being younger may make an individual more likely to participate in an ALMP in Canada as a whole, when looking at an individual province or territory, this may no longer be the case. In this way, the individual's characteristics have the potential to influence the propensity score differently in all the separate regional estimates.

An additional practical step that ESDC might like to consider on specification checking is comparing their results broken down into PTs to the estimate derived for the whole of Canada. By combining all of the separate estimates for PTs into an average, it is possible to recreate the results for Canada. It is not expected that this re-created Canadian average would be identical to the separate estimate for the whole of Canada, due to previously mentioned point that the variables in the separate regional models can influence the propensity score differently in a regional model. However, there should be a broad concordance between the combination of the estimates for the PTs and the aggregate Canada estimate. Where this is not the case it may be evidence of some kind of mis-specification.

For example, when combining the regional estimates for impact on incidence of employment of Employment Assistance Services, it is difficult to reconcile them with the estimate for Canada. Separate estimates are produced by ESDC for nine of the thirteen PTs. Four PTs do not have separate estimates-Quebec does not take part in the joint evaluation and Northwest Territories, Nunavut and Yukon do not have separate figures reported in the evaluation results. Figure 4.2 shows the average that is needed for these, for the weighted average of all PTs to equal that of the separately estimated figure for Canada. It is negative in sign, in contrast to all of the other individual estimates. This suggests that, unless there is an unusual effect of the programme in those four PTs, there may be some kind of specification error in either the estimate for Canada, or some of the individual PTs. This may warrant further investigation of what is going on for these estimates. By conducting this type of assessment more routinely, ESDC could make a virtue of having the separate PTs estimates and perform a more in-depth assessment of model specification.

Specification checking could also be supplemented with a "test-train" procedure. Here the original dataset is split randomly into two, the first dataset is used to estimate the propensity scores. The model estimated from this is then applied to the second dataset. If the model is able to successfully balance the individual characteristics and produce participants and non-participants that are alike, then it is further evidence that the model is well specified and fits the population more generally, rather than being "over-fitted" to the specific individuals that happen to appear in the first dataset.

Figure 4.2. Individual PTs estimates for EAS incidence of employment impacts imply a significantly negative impact for those PTs without an individual assessment

Employment Assistance Services (EAS), impact on incidence of employment by region, active claimants

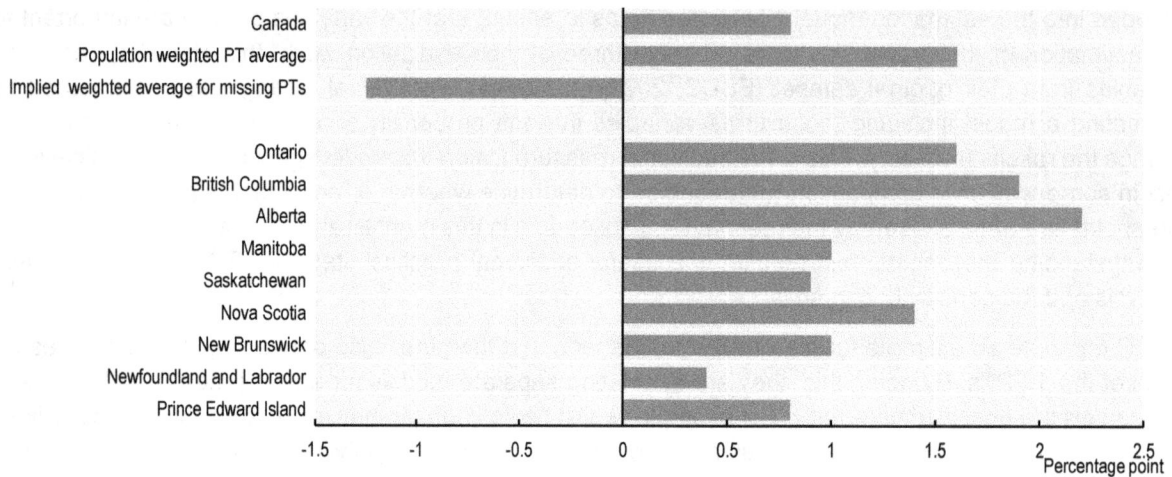

PTs: Provinces and Territories.
Note: Weighted average derived using sample sizes detailed in the individual reports. Random samples of data were used for Canada, Alberta, British Colombia, Manitoba and Ontario- these have been scaled up to population levels. Quebec sample size estimated as Canada minus sum of the individual PTs. "Missing PTs" is the combination of Quebec, Northwest Territories, Nunavut and Yukon.
Source: Individual Employment and Social Development Canada ESDC impact assessment reports on provinces and territories (2017-2018), available at www.canada.ca.

StatLink 〓 https://stat.link/cxls3f

Individuals without a similar comparator are removed from analysis

Matching also requires that the participants and non-participants have a potential individual that looks sufficiently like them in their propensity to participate in the programme. For example, if there is a participant in the programme with a very strong probability of participation and a propensity score of 0.9 and no similar individual exists in the non-participant group, then it is necessary to remove that individual from the matching process. This is because there is no individual sufficiently alike to them and therefore it is not possible to adequately match an individual that could reliably provide a comparison to what outcome the participant would enjoyed had they not participated. ESDC conduct this assessment via a graphical inspection of the distribution plots, which is a standard technique in the literature (Caliendo and Kopeinig, 2008[24]). This allows to ensure the matching begins with an appropriate set of participant and non-participants.

Different types of matching algorithm are assessed

Once a propensity score has been estimated, there are various different algorithms that may be used to match individuals to one another (and so create the participant and non-participant groups) with this score. Whilst an in-depth technical assessment of these algorithms is beyond the scope of this paper, the general principles of testing are interesting to discuss. ESDC use kernel density matching as the technique for their central impact assessments. However, estimates were also made using inverse probability weighting, nearest neighbour and cross-sectional matching (ESDC, 2021[23]). The results displayed demonstrate that outcome estimates are not sensitive to the choice of matching algorithm that is used. In this case it provides re-assurance that results are not driven by the choice of the algorithm used to match the data. One point to bring out of these tests is that it may be preferable from a computational point of view to implement the matching by inverse probability weighting, rather than kernel density matching, given that the former is faster to implement because it requires less computation power. Indeed, this is a conclusion that was reached in an earlier assessment of the LMDA analysis (Handouyahia, Haddad and Eaton, 2013[25])

Checks are made on the stability of the relationships between participants and non-participants over time

ESDC also conducts checks to determine whether the DID estimates conform to the assumption that differences between participants and non-participants are stable over time. Analysis of these trends suggests that there is a good stability on the difference between them, after matching has taken place (ESDC, 2021[23]). Participant and non-participant earnings are charted over time, however it is difficult to gauge differences visually on the aggregate annual earnings measure displayed in the ESDC reports (ESDC, 2021[23]). Further charts, which display the difference between the earnings of the participants and non-participants rather than their absolute levels, would be beneficial in this respect. To formalise this further, statistical tests can be conducted, using an event study set-up. Rather than test whether a programme has a significant impact on earnings using the difference in pre- and post-programme periods of participants, differences between participants and non-participants are also tested statistically before the participation. The period before the programme is usually broken down into disaggregated periods (the annual data that ESDC use would suggest years for a breakdown in their work). If annual data are used, this would then test whether differences in earnings are significant in each year prior to the programme period. If no statistically significant differences are found on the earnings of participants and non-participants in the period before participation then it provides evidence that there is a stable relationship over time between them. Kauhanen and Virtanen (2021[26]) provide a recent example in a study on adult education policy in Finland (including charts where differences are charted rather than levels).

ESDC conducts methodical and extensive statistical data checks which cover all of the main areas that a robust check of statistical analysis should comprise. There are small improvement and tweaks that ESDC may consider. For example, further investigation into differences at the PTs level analysis may provide additional information, outside of formal statistical testing, on how well specified their models are and would make further use of work they have already conducted for other reasons. These tests are produced in a technical report for the LMDA evaluation (ESDC, 2021[23]), but also turning them into a non-technical passage and incorporating them in the executive summary of non-technical reports may assist a broader audience in understanding some of the strengths and inherent uncertainties of the existing approach.

4.4. Cost-benefit analysis

To assess the value for money of a policy, consideration also needs to be given to the costs of provision and to wider benefits, which may occur indirectly. An ALMP may be successful in helping a person into work, but if the cost of doing so outweighs the extra benefit from that person entering work then it will not be cost-effective to proceed with the policy. Despite the advances in analytical techniques and the number of ALMPs that are now evaluated, detailed cost-benefit analyses are still rare (Card, Kluve and Weber, 2018[7]). Canada is an exemplar in this respect and sets out a clear and comprehensive cost-benefit analysis of its ALMPs that facilitates informed discussion of their relative merits. Explicitly incorporating both the costs and the benefits of participation into an assessment of value means that it has a much better basis to evaluate programmes than viewing the benefits in isolation (as is more routine in impact assessment). It also brings in wider dimensions of government finance, such as tax and wider benefits, than a narrow focus on labour market outcomes.

4.4.1. Data on costs are important to properly contextualise benefits

A comprehensive estimate of all of the costs of provision of a programme, including those incurred indirectly, is required to feed into a thorough cost-benefit assessment. In some cases, savings elsewhere might offset costs of programme provision. For example, a training programme that gets people into work quickly may mean that public employment services also spend less money on a counsellor to help them find a job. Similarly, benefits may be wider than the income gain to the participant. The use of wider social services, such as health care, and the impact on crime might also be considered. There is a secondary link to government finances directly via taxation receipt, as this just represents a transfer from one individual to another, it does not impact upon primary cost-benefit calculations. However, it may be useful to consider for public finance discussions. Consideration of the impact of a programme on government spending, in light of the distortionary impact that ad valorem taxation has on behaviour, should also be taken account of. A programme that causes a net increase to government spending will increase negative distortions to behaviour (for example, government spending that necessitates a higher income tax to pay for it might mean that fewer individuals choose to work, or reduce their hours of work).

ESDC adds costs to its analysis and looks at value for money through a range of lenses

In order to evaluate the cost-benefit of the LMDAs, ESDC begins with its estimates from the counterfactual impact assessment and then adds a number of elements to complete the analysis (Table 4.4). All of the assessment is done at the individual level, comparing the costs of delivering the programme to the individual compared to the benefits that the individual receives as a result. There are three different accounting units that are considered in this framework:

- Individual – this looks at all changes that are only relevant to the person participating. Programme costs and social costs of public funds are not relevant to the individual so are not included. The change to employment earnings is a large component of this calculation. Income and sales taxes paid by the individual enter as a negative figure. The receipt of social assistance and employment insurance may enter as a positive or negative depending on whether the individual receives more or less of them as a result.

- Government – looks at how changes relate to government finances. For example, programme costs and social costs of public funds enter the calculation negatively. Income and sales taxes received by government are positive. The change to employment earnings does not enter the government calculation, except where it changes the income taxes paid, because that benefit accrues directly to the individual.

- Social – accounts for impact of the changes on society. The important thing here is that changes to employment earnings enter the calculation, as they increase or decrease output in the economy. Changes to government taxation receipt and benefit receipt are not entered in the calculation because they represent a transfer from government to the individual, so there is no net gain to society.

Whilst the investment decision for a programme should be based upon the social impact, because this provides the answer on whether a dollar invested provides more or less than that to society, it is useful to consider the individual and government accounting units. Viewing the programme through the lens of an individual provides a better perspective on the decisions that an individual is making when deciding upon participation in a programme (and could be used by public employment services when advertising the benefits of a programme to potential participants). Consideration of the government perspective allows a focus to be given to public financing, that may be useful when considering the political economy on whether or not to invest into a programme (although a first-best decision by a finance ministry should take into account the social returns, there can often by constraints on financing, particularly where a programme might take some time to repay its investment).

In order to calculate the returns to those different groups, ESDC brings in a number of additional estimates to its impact analysis. On the benefit side, changes in employment income, social assistance and employment insurance receipt are taken directly from the counterfactual impact assessment. An estimate for how this affects payment of sales tax is then derived from looking at the changes in employment income and calculating how much of this will be spent, at the prevailing average provincial and federal sales tax rates.

On the cost side, estimates are constructed using administrative accounting data on aggregate delivery costs. These are split into operational and administrative costs. Operational costs take the total direct administrative expenditure of providing a programme divided by the number of those programmes delivered, to estimate the cost of delivering that programme to an individual. Administrative costs comprise the ancillary spending and overheads necessary to administer the programme (for example ESDC staff that co-ordinate and manage the ALMPs). They are not available per programme and so the estimate is made by taking the total and splitting this into programme type based on that programme's relative share of the operational costs (for example, if operational costs of Targeted Wage Subsidies were 30% of total spending on operational costs across all programmes, it would also constitute 30% of total administrative costs. An estimate of the social cost of public funds is then calculated (this enters Table 4.4 as a cost only because the ALMP involves net government spending. If a programme directly saved government money then it would be a benefit to the programme). Following expert advice, the amount of this cost is estimated as 20% of the net change to government spending (the cost of providing the programme and the net change to tax receipts). This is comparable to estimates made in other government assessments of its potential role in impact assessment (Fujiwara (2010[27]), Australian Department of Finance and Administration (2006[28]))

Table 4.4. ESDC consider a number of costs and benefits in addition to the counterfactual impact evaluation

Benefits	Costs
Employment income	Programme costs (operational and administrative)
Fringe benefits – Employer-paid health and life insurance, pension contributions	Social cost of public funds
Income and Sales taxes	
Receipt of social assistance and employment insurance	

Source: ESDC (2016[29]), "Cost-Benefit Analysis of Employment Benefits and Support Measures".

Costs and benefits are then brought to a common base for comparison

Once costs and benefits have been estimated, the last stage is to account for the fact that some costs and benefits fall into different years. This is known as discounting and cost-benefit estimates that have been discounted are in a "net present value". This means all the figures can be compared as if they occurred in the current time period. It reduces the weight of values in later years relative to earlier ones. Costs and benefits in the central estimate are added up over six years following the programme, and for two years during programme participation. The rate at which this is set for ESDC is 5% per annum. This means a USD 100 benefit (or cost) earned in one year's time is only valued at USD 95.2 (100/1.05). If this USD 100 had been earned in two years' time, it would be worth USD 90.7 (100/(1.05*10.5)). ESDC set this rate to account for two factors: inflation and interest foregone on government investment. Foregone government investment accounts for the fact that the government could have instead invested the money elsewhere and earnt money on this investment. Discounting is important to ensure that costs and benefits that occur over time are compared on the same basis.

4.4.2. Some known costs and benefits are not yet included in the assessment

There are wider costs and benefits that are not considered in the ESDC cost-benefit analysis but would be beneficial to consider. These are explicitly referenced in the ESDC report (ESDC, 2016[29]):

- Intangible benefits to mental health and physical well-being
- Effects on crime

- Multiplier effects – where increased employment and spending in the economy generates further increases in employment and spending
- Displacement effects – where participants take jobs away from non-participants

Incorporation of health data, to estimate what impact ALMPs have on the health-related expenditure of individuals, will help to better contextualise all of the gains from the LMDA. Empirical research has shown that higher income can lead to better health outcomes (Benzeval and Judge, 2001[30]). Raising employment therefore has the potential to reduce health care spending. Employment policies that specifically target lower-income individuals can therefore play a vital role in supporting health care systems. ESDC are currently working on the incorporation of estimates of the impact of ALMPs on health outcomes to the analysis. This will provide a better understanding of the additional secondary benefits that ALMPs can have and a richer understanding on the impacts of ALMPs on individuals.

Similarly, adding the effects of ALMPs on subsequent crime rates, with their associated costs to society, would complement the existing analysis. Grogger (1998[31]) provides an estimate from the United States that looks at changes to propensity to commit crime due to changes in income. Incorporating this into an estimate on the reductions to crime via the increased income from ALMPs would then be straightforward. In combination with estimates for the cost of crime, this could then be incorporating into the cost-benefit assessment.

Providing evidence on displacement effects is difficult to achieve using ESDC's current evaluation strategy. It relies on estimating the impact on the employment that participants of a programme have on the employment prospects of non-participants. Indeed non-participants are the very individuals that are used to estimate the overall programme effects. If displacement was occurring, it would cause an overestimate of the beneficial effects of the programme, because the non-participant employment rate (or level of earnings) would be lower, directly causing the estimate of the programme to improve. This may be more likely to affect Employment Assistance Services because transitions into work are quicker and greater in volume than other programmes (relative to say a training programme, for which the participation period can be a number of months), meaning it has more potential to affect the job-finding of non-participants. A study in Sweden is an example of where a carefully planned randomised trial may help to provide evidence (Cheung et al., 2019[32]). The study took place across 72 randomly selected public employment service offices in Sweden. Of these 72, 36 were randomly selected to the treatment programme. Within each office, jobseekers were randomly assigned to the programme. This two stage randomisation of offices and jobseekers, was implemented so that displacement effects could be estimated. Estimates of displacement were made by comparing non-participants in offices with the programme to non-participants in offices without the programme. It showed that such displacement was present in job counselling services, suggesting it is an area that merits further attention.

Distributional weighting is an area which is not covered in ESDC's existing cost-benefit analysis, but which might be worth considering as an addition to it. Distributional weighting increases or decreases the value of a programme to an individual based on how rich or poor that individual is. It is based on the idea that it is desirable to reflect the differences in marginal benefit of consumption between rich and poor individuals, particularly pertinent for the LMDA as they are delivered to individuals lower down the income distribution. This uses the concept of diminishing marginal returns to consumption, so that a dollar spent by a poor individual is "worth" more to them than a dollar spent by a rich person is to them. The United Kingdom advises that weighting is considered where redistribution is an explicit policy aim, such as in welfare payments (HM Treasury, 2020[33]). The Australian guidance is slightly more equivocal and only advocates any sort of weighting approach where an unambiguous policy objective is identified to assist a specific group, to avoid subjective biases in weighting (Department of Finance and Administration, 2006[28]). However, social policy would fall under the scope of such a requirement. By presenting distributional weighting alongside the standard CBA assessments, it would allow ESDC to better contextualise the policies and secure ALMPs budgets.

4.4.3. Sensitivity analysis is conducted to demonstrate the uncertainty of estimates

In addition to its core estimates, ESDC provides sensitivity analysis on three variables used in the construct of the cost-benefit analysis. It alters each of the following variables one by one (and in combination with one another) to analyse the impact they have on the cost-benefit estimate. The three variables it alters are:

- Discount rate – varying it to 3% and 7%.
- Marginal social cost of public funds – varying it to 0% and 50%.
- Length of impacts considered – extrapolating impacts in year six out to 15 and 25 years

The inclusion of sensitivity analysis is welcome and should be commended, as it helps to display the uncertainty around the estimates, which depend on several different assumptions. It conducts combinations of these three adjustments (so that there are 27 cost-benefit estimates, including the original central estimate). These sensitivity variations have been conducted using expert judgements.

Some additions to the sensitivity analysis would aid discussion of its likely range and central estimate

An important addition to the sensitivity analysis would be to allow variation to the estimated impacts on earnings, social assistance and employment insurance (aside from extending the length for which they are accounted for). The estimates arising from the quantitative DID analysis will have been accompanied with "standard errors", which provide information on how much uncertainty there is around each central estimates. This provides a natural candidate for which to use in sensitivity, to increase and decrease the central estimates by in the sensitivity analysis.

It is possible to extend the sensitivity testing of the cost-benefit analysis further using statistical Monte Carlo simulations. This helps to give more insight into how combinations of variable variations may group together and gives more information on where sensitivity estimates are grouped (for example, whether they are spread equally over a range, whether more of them are under the central estimate or above it). In this work possible values for variables ("distributions") have to be chosen for each of the variable that is being varied (New Zealand Treasury, 2015[34]). At their simplest, they could take the form of a triangular distribution (where a variable can take three values, a low, medium and high), not dissimilar to the variations already conducted by ESDC. For variables for which there are more empirical data available, more complex distributions could be chosen (for example, on the discount rate by looking at previous inflation and government bond time series to estimate an appropriate distribution). Monte Carlo works by then repeatedly picking a value for each of the variables, based on their underlying distributions, and then computing the resulting cost-benefit. By repeating this action thousands of time, the process itself produces a distribution of cost-benefit estimates.

Overall, the work that Canada conducts on cost-benefit analysis is comprehensive and rigorous. It permits a much more detailed evaluation of the relative pros and cons of its ALMPs. It also demonstrates that with a clear framework and rationale for cost-benefit analysis, a relatively comprehensive assessment can be achieved without too many additional steps over and above a more narrow impact assessment. At a minimum, incorporating the costs of programme provision and calculating the extra taxes and benefits paid by individuals, all in their net present value, allows a good basic cost-benefit analysis to be conducted, which permits a much more rounded discussion of programme merits than in their absence. The additional in-direct impacts on health, crime and distortions relating to government financing can then supplement this further.

4.5. Analytical delivery: In-house or out-sourced

The choice over whether to deliver ALMP evaluations in-house or via external contractors is a multi-faceted one and countries have different approaches, many opting for some combination of both. ESDC has invested in an analytical capability, housed within its Evaluation Directorate, to conduct all of the required ALMP evaluations internally, transforming a delivery system that previously relied upon external contractors to deliver. This section discusses some of the choices that are relevant to these strategies, offering insight into the advantages and disadvantages of different strategies and provides examples from the Canadian setting.

Once a decision has been made to evaluate ALMPs in a country, three broad strategies exist:

- In-house – e.g. Australia, Canada;
- Out-sourced – e.g. Denmark, Finland;
- A combination of in-house and outsourced – e.g. Estonia, France, Germany, New Zealand, Sweden, Switzerland, United Kingdom.

Conducting evaluations in-house or by contracting-out depends largely on decisions around the required expertise to conduct analysis, the possibility to make data available to external partners, the frequency of such studies, the capacity to manage external research projects and the capacity to manage the narrative from the analysis.

Those ministries that have smaller, or no, analytical functions may be better placed to contract-out research, rather than having a dedicated evaluation function. For example, The Ministry of Economic Affairs and Employment in Finland made the decision to rationalise its previous evaluation function as part of a drive to focus resource on day-to-day policy delivery and retains only a small team of analysts to serve ministerial business. It instead chooses to out-source its delivery of evaluation. This contrasts to the evaluation directorate in ESDC which shifted to a strategy of conducting this type of evaluation work in-house, so that ESDC can more easily ring-fence specialist resource for evaluation.

Some countries navigate these issues using a "quasi-in-house" research institute- such as the Institute for Employment Research in Germany or the Institute for Evaluation of Labour Market and Education Policy in Sweden. These institutes are external to the employment ministry and allow research expertise to coalesce around specific mandates for analysis. This separation is useful to ensure resources are devoted to analytical assessment of public policy, ring-fencing them from divergence within ministries to other policy development priorities. They can also serve as a data warehousing and access body that can facilitate the wider sharing of their data with external researchers. This happens at both of the institutes mentioned.

Legislative requirements to evaluate, as happens in Germany and Sweden, as well as in Canada, are useful to ensure open and transparent assessment of policy (see OECD (2020[35]) for a discussion of developments). It avoids the political "cherry picking" of policy analysis- only choosing to evaluate policies that are convenient to a particular political narrative at the time. Those countries without legislative mandates to evaluate policy and who do not open data up to external researchers risk ad hoc and piecemeal policy assessment. Even countries that do offer open data access, without legislative evaluation requirements, risk their evaluations following the same path, if data and analysis is not suitably accessible and demanded enough by the wider research community. For example, whilst Finland offers researchers access to high-quality microeconomic data on its ALMPs, that in principle mean that they could be assessed in observational studies, it still lacks evidence on some of its programmes. Concerted efforts from policy makers, external pressure groups or research communities to ensure assessments are prioritised, can help countries to ensure that policy evaluation does not remain incomplete.

4.5.1. Impact evaluation in ESDC is carried out in-house

ESDC moved capacity to conduct impact evaluations in-house after the first iteration of summative evaluations of the LMDA were completed. The driving force behind this move was a desire to increase responsiveness of analysis to policy and utilise administrative data to increase precision of estimates and to reduce costs. Whilst the use of contractors to analyse administrative data could have been facilitated, there are additional benefits for internal analysts to conduct such work. It is easier for them to collaborate with internal colleagues who have knowledge on the existing data that is housed within the department. It also offers wider spill-over effects within the organisation, particularly when staff move into different but related analytical roles- they retain their knowledge of the data and its structure and can bring this to bear in new analytical projects. Over the years, ESDC has built up a store of analytical expertise centred on knowledge transfer via individuals and knowledge retention via extensive documentation of data, code and techniques.

Expertise was developed primarily through two distinct teams. One with a remit to create analytical datasets to use for evaluation and conduct rigorous econometric techniques to these data to estimate causal impacts of programmes offered and another to manage the process of engagement with PTs and qualitative data collection (see Chapter 2, Section 2.4.2 for more detail). This distinction allowed resources to specialise to deliver policy analysis at a faster pace and with greater precision. With the support of ESDC Chief Data Office, the data team focused on the inclusion of the CRA data into an integrated evaluation dataset and proceed with the quantitative work and the other team worked on "regional" issues, liaising with PTs to ensure that analytical requirements for data were well understood, that the underlying data transfers from PTs reliably captured those requirements and conducting the required qualitative work. The relationships built up with PTs by the data team made them the natural home to manage these ESDC-PTs interactions. As resource increased over time, further specialisation was made possible, including separation of resource to manage data processing; to advise on methodology and quality assurance; and to conduct analysis (see Chapter 2 for more details).

Reducing costs of delivery was one of the drivers for the change behind the shift to in-house administrative data led evaluations. Costs of external contractors were reduced from around CAD 1 million per annum to CAD 70 000 (Gingras et al., 2017[36]). However, it is unclear the extent to which in-house delivery of the quantitative evaluation work alone was responsible for this. The major methodological change of using integrated administrative data is likely to be the primary driver of reductions in costs (via avoidance of the associated costs of data collection via surveys). Unless productivity is sufficiently higher in the public sector, the cost of conducting evaluation should be broadly equivalent between the internal/contracted-out delivery methods- favouring government only via its lower financing costs (borrowing at the risk-free interest rate rather than private sector equity-debt rates).

One of the benefits of moving analysis in-house has been the consistency of the analysis and the continuity of the work. It has allowed ESDC to build a set of analytical processes and resources that is fully adapted to ESDC needs and is flexible to its requirements. The increased resources allocated by the Evaluation Directorate over time reflected, in part, the increase demand for the conduct of this type of analysis internally and for other ESDC active labour market programs. It has also freed up internal resources whose main tasked involved the management of processes to select contractors and the following contract, as well as the management and review of their deliverables. This means that resources can be focussed on conducting evaluation activities instead.

The building blocks to develop high-class internally delivered ALMP evaluations

The cyclical framework adopted by ESDC has also allowed it to develop a pathway for evaluation that contains key steps in ensuring that analysis is continuously developed and can be refined and adapted based on evolving needs and updated evidence. Figure 4.3 uses the ROAMEF framework, which categorises policy development into stages covering Rationale, Objectives, Appraisal, Monitoring,

Evaluation and Feedback. It is useful for breaking down the process and visualising it as an iterative set of interconnected processes, though it is important to note this is not intended to convey a completely linear set of relationships and connections can flow between all of the individual processes (HM Treasury, 2020[37]). This illustrates how the different sets of processes and procedures that ESDC has developed have contributed to its development of programme evaluation. The delineation of analysis into discrete cycles allows ESDC to ensure it consistently iterates its objectives and deliverables based on the results from the previous wave of evaluation. In this manner, it formalises the process for renewal of these and provides natural break-points for the programme of work. This is evident when viewing the existing three cycles next to one another; the first based upon bilateral survey-based analysis; the second augmenting this with simultaneous administrative data-based analysis; the third re-focussing towards sub-group analysis using machine-learning. The internal delivery of analysis allows the analytical teams to be part of this entire cycle, facilitating responsiveness to changing evaluation needs and ensuring flexibility in planning and delivery of the work.

Figure 4.3. ESDC undertakes a number of steps to assure and iterate analysis

Procedures displayed within the ROAMEF framework

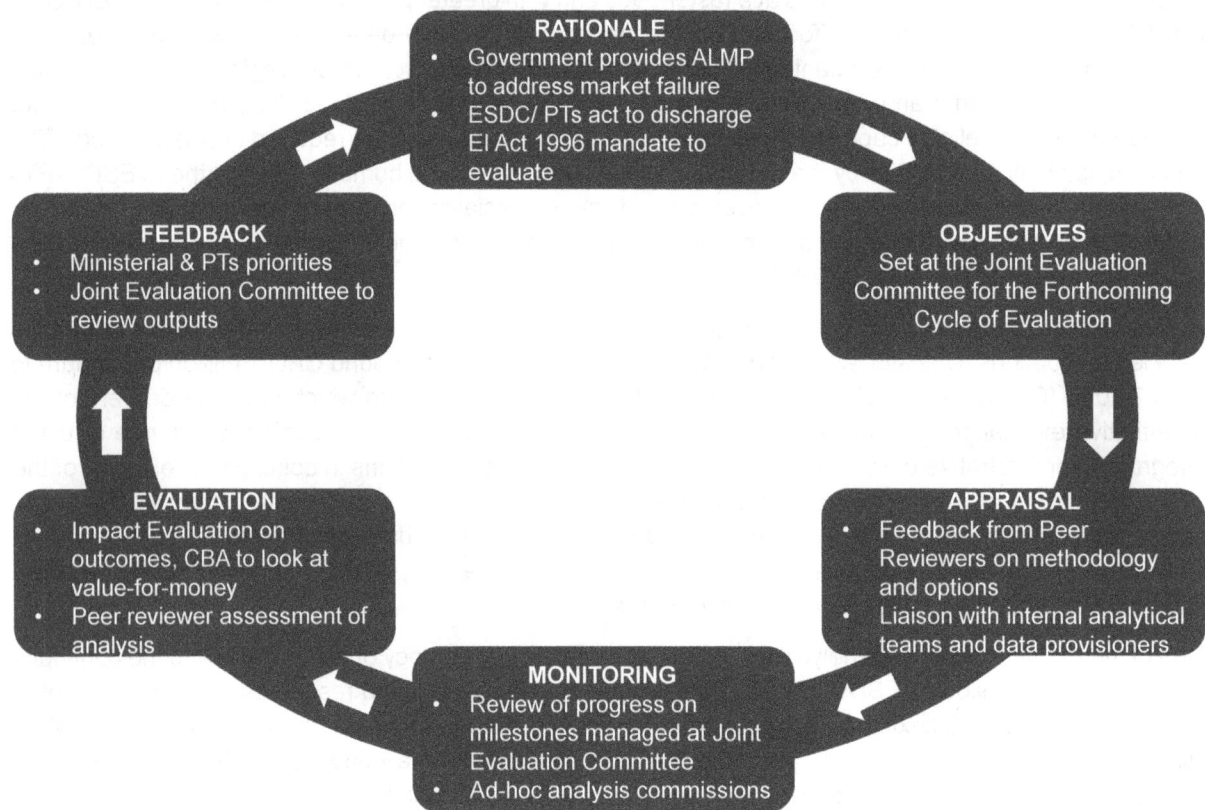

Source: Authors illustration, adapted from H M Treasury (2020[37]), Magenta Book Central Government guidance on evaluation, https://www.gov.uk/government/publications/the-magenta-book.

4.6. Peer review

In order to supplement analysis where needed, provide guidance and add additional scrutiny and quality assurance to the work, ESDC have employed a number of external academic experts. These experts lend both expert judgement and credibility to the programme of evaluation.

At the outset of the move towards in-house delivery, the production of a report to provide recommendations into the methodological requirements for evaluation of the LMDAs, was externally commissioned to guide the second stage of the evaluation (Smith, 2008[38]). The report set out the rationale for evaluation, the key research questions and suggestions on the outcomes to evaluate and the techniques to use in this evaluation. It formed the basis of the techniques utilised by ESDC in subsequent analysis and ensured that ESDC had a solid analytical platform from which to build its analytical resources. This was especially important at the beginning of their transition to in-house methodology, before expertise had really been built up internally into a sustained and established function.

ESDC have then continued to conduct peer reviews of their evaluations and reports, utilising contractual arrangements with three leading academics in the field of ALMPs.[3] These reviews offer insight into the methodologies used and the writing up of results into reports. Having three independent sources of input allows ESDC to benefit from a wide-ranging but extremely technical assessment of their policy evaluation strategies and methodology. The assessment mostly comes in the form of written comments on ESDC evaluation reports. This peer review process has also given ESDC the ability to verify the recommendations from the report which guided the second stage of LMDA evaluations and to further develop and refine the ESDC's evaluation strategy. Box 4.3 provides some examples from the United Kingdom into how the communication of these peer reviews might be better shared with the general public and further support the credibility of the analysis. It also provides suggestions about how better strategic links with the academic may be fostered, to better inform future evidence-making. The use of an advisory group, with different analytical specialisms, may be interesting to consider. ESDC have largely employed economists, who will offer similar professional perspectives than had a wider range of scientific disciplines been consulted.

One of the key features of the ESDC peer review system, has been the development of long-standing relationships with their main peer reviewers. This allows the peer reviewers to build a detailed and historically enriched view of the Canadian system, so that they too can develop their quality assurance over time, building on their previous assessments and their own institutional knowledge. At the same time this brings risks over future proofing, if these relationships cease to exist. This kind of knowledge becomes more difficult to institutionalise than if it existed internally to ESDC. The presence and retention of the previous assessments mitigates this risk somewhat.

Having a standardised template for peer reviews, with sections on the different aspects of the evaluation that have been reviewed (for example, the data, techniques, outcomes evaluated and the assessment of their use, advantages and shortcomings) and publishing summaries of them alongside the final ESDC evaluation reports would give greater confidence to the results reported, as it would allow the public to explicitly see how experts in the field appraise ESDC's work and have confidence in the results (see (BIS, 2015[39]) for an example of where this is done in the United Kingdom).

The peer reviewers have not been in a position to scrutinise the underlying data and code used to produce results, which is not unusual for this type of assessment. But it does mean there is a primacy for this to be done correctly as part of ESDCs usual analytical processes. Peer reviewers cannot provide verification of the underlying analysis, but they require sufficient documentation to comment on analysis and outputs, provide guidance on at least part of the analytical structure and clarity (as it pertains to communicating results). Most importantly for this part of the quality assurance, they provide validation of the techniques and methods and on the underlying data and methodology.

Box 4.3. Put more peer in your review

The Department for Work and Pensions (DWP) in the United Kingdom offers practical examples that can increase trust and make best use of academic peer reviewers to inform policy analysis:

- **Methods Advisory Group** – Is an expert panel in the DWP consisting of external specialists from several different scientific disciplines with the express intention of supporting the Chief Scientific Advisor to utilise cutting-edge scientific, technical and analytical approaches to generate robust evidence on analytical questions. In practice this group can be consulted prior to undertaking any research to offer advice on intended data and methodological approach. That its membership is diverse across the sciences allows cross-fertilisation of ideas to help avoid group-think. Individual members with specific subject expertise have also built up bilateral links with their relevant policy makers, to take advantage of more informal knowledge sharing. Applications to join the group are voluntary and appointments are made by open advertisement.

- **Areas of Research Interest** – GO Science supports ministries to publish a summary of their core strategic research questions. This allows an open and transparent communication with academics, that allows them to structure their research proposals to areas of the government's ministries and opens the path for future debate between policy makers and academics. The DWP has utilised their framework to embark on a series of national seminars taking place at universities, where government and academic researchers present work based around these themes. The idea being to foster further links between the DWP and the research communities.

- **PhD placements** – DWP also participates in a broader government scheme to bring PhD students into the department for short periods- around three months- to work on specific research questions. The scheme is meant to be mutually beneficial to the department and individuals- giving the former access to extra, specialised resources to answer specific research questions and the latter experience in using rich, administrative data and practical implementation of the skills they have acquired. It has the additional benefit of further embedding the links between government and academia that the department has been developing. This is facilitated through a broader scheme run by the Open Innovation team, a team that sits within the Cabinet Office with a remit to generate analysis and ideas for policy by working with external experts.

ESDC already have informal engagement and good links with some universities, so are benefitting from some of these engagements already. However, proceeding on a more formalised basis may further encourage innovation and would open up opportunity to candidates for placements, and for academics research interests, in a wider range of universities on a more systematic basis.

Source: Methods Advisory Group, https://www.gov.uk/government/groups/dwp-methods-advisory-group; Areas of Research Interest, https://www.gov.uk/government/collections/areas-of-research-interest; PhD placements, https://openinnovation.blog.gov.uk/wp-content/uploads/sites/214/2020/10/OiT_PhD_Recruitment.pdf.

4.7. Summary

ESDC has made virtue of rich administrative data to conduct high-quality analysis of ALMPs using observational studies. It ensures that participants and non-participants are alike using a combination of techniques. The virtue of this is that it can use the administrative data available to construct pools of similar participants and non-participants and supplement this with a method that also controls for differences between individuals that do not change over time. Considering whether to supplement this analysis with well-designed randomised tests at the PTs level, would allow ESDC to look at more detailed questions on programme design and the best mode of delivery. A range of work is undertaken to demonstrate that the statistical models chosen are not sensitive to the variables they contain. Some extensions to testing, building on already disaggregated PTs reporting, would allow even further investigation in questions of model specification. Diagnostics tests are also performed to ensure that the estimates conform to the underlying assumptions necessary for them to provide robust results, such as ensuring participant and non-participants are alike and that differences between them are stable over time.

ESDC performs a thorough cost-benefit analysis, employing data on costs to properly contextualise the impacts of programmes. This could be extended further with incorporation of data on health and more work to vary assumptions to demonstrate uncertainty. All of this analysis is performed in-house, with expertise developed over the years by ESDC. In addition to internal analytical teams, ESDC uses expert external peer reviews to provide scrutiny and credibility to this work.

References

Arni, P. (2011), *Langzeitarbeitslosigkeit verhindern: Intensivberatung und Coaching für ältere Stellensuchende.* [19]

Arni, P. et al. (2013), *L'impact des réseaux sociaux sur le retour à l'emploi des chômeurs*, State Secretariat for Economic Affairs SECO, https://www.seco.admin.ch/seco/en/home/Publikationen_Dienstleistungen/Publikationen_und_Formulare/Arbeit/Arbeitsmarkt/Informationen_Arbeitsmarktforschung/l_impact-des-reseaux-sociaux-sur-le-retour-a-lemploi-des-chomeur.html. [20]

Arni, P. and A. Schiprowski (2015), *Die Rolle von Erwartungshaltungen in der Stellensuche und der RAV-Beratung (Teilprojekt 2): Der Jobchancen-Barometer und die Erwartungshaltungen der Personalberatenden*, https://www.iza.org/publications/r/178/die-rolle-von-erwartungshaltungen-in-der-stellensuche-und-der-rav-beratung-teilprojekt-2-pilotprojekt-jobchancen-barometer. [21]

Benzeval, M. and K. Judge (2001), "Income and health: the time dimension", *Social Science & Medicine*, Vol. 52/9, pp. 1371-1390, https://doi.org/10.1016/S0277-9536(00)00244-6. [30]

BIS (2015), "BIS Evaluation Summary and Peer Review Title: Measuring the Net Present Value of Further Education in England", https://www.gov.uk/government/publications/further-education-comparing- (accessed on 14 October 2021). [39]

Boll, J. et al. (2013), *Evaluering På rette vej - i job*, https://star.dk/media/1309/paa-rette-vej-i-job-evaluering.pdf. [17]

Boll, J. and M. Hertz (2009), *Aktive Hurtigere tilbarge*, https://star.dk/media/1358/aktive-hurtigere-tilbage-implementering-og-deltageroplevelse.pdf. [16]

Caliendo, M. and S. Kopeinig (2008), "Some practical guidance for the implementation of propensity score matching", *Journal of Economic Surveys*, Vol. 22/1, pp. 31-72, https://doi.org/10.1111/j.1467-6419.2007.00527.x. [24]

Card, D., J. Kluve and A. Weber (2018), "What Works? A Meta Analysis of Recent Active Labor Market Program Evaluations", *Journal of the European Economic Association*, Vol. 16/3, pp. 894-931, https://doi.org/10.1093/JEEA/JVX028. [7]

Cheung, M. et al. (2019), "Does Job Search Assistance Reduce Unemployment? Experimental Evidence on Displacement Effects and Mechanisms", *SSRN Electronic Journal*, https://doi.org/10.2139/SSRN.3515935. [32]

Department of Finance and Administration (2006), *Handbook of Cost Benefit Analysis*, Commonwealth of Australia, https://www.pmc.gov.au/sites/default/files/files/handbook-of-cb-analysis-2006.pdf. [28]

DiNardo, J. and D. Lee (2011), "Program Evaluation and Research Designs", in *Handbook of Labor Economics*, Elsevier, https://doi.org/10.1016/s0169-7218(11)00411-4. [2]

ESDC (2021), *Analysis of Employment Benefits and Support Measures (EBSM) Profile and Medium-Term Incremental Impacts from 2010 to 2017*, Employment and Social Development Canada (unpublished). [23]

ESDC (2019), *Quantitative Methodology Report – Final*, Employment and Social Development Canada (unpublished). [8]

ESDC (2016), *Cost-Benefit Analysis of Employment Benefits and Support Measures*, Employment and Social Development Canada, https://publications.gc.ca/site/eng/9.834566/publication.html. [29]

Fujiwara D (2010), *The Department for Work and Pensions Social Cost-Benefit Analysis framework: Methodologies for estimating and incorporating the wider social and economic impacts of work in Cost-Benefit Analysis of Employment Programmes*, Department for Work and Pensions, United Kingdom, https://assets.publishing.service.gov.uk/government/uploads/system/uploads/attachment_data/file/214384/WP86.pdf. [27]

Gingras, Y. et al. (2017), "Making Evaluation More Responsive to Policy Needs: The Case of the Labour Market Development Agreements", *Canadian Journal of Program Evaluation*, Vol. 32/2, https://doi.org/10.3138/cjpe.31119. [36]

Grogger, J. (1998), "Market Wages and Youth Crime", *Journal of Labor Economics*, Vol. 16/4, pp. 756-791, https://doi.org/10.1086/209905. [31]

Handouyahia, A., T. Haddad and F. Eaton (2013), *Kernel Matching versus Inverse Probability Weighting: A Comparative Study*, International Journal of Mathematical and Computational Sciences, https://publications.waset.org/16101/pdf. [25]

Heckman, J., R. Lalonde and J. Smith (1999), "The Economics and Econometrics of Active Labor Market Programs", in *Handbook of Labor Economics*, Elsevier, https://doi.org/10.1016/s1573-4463(99)03012-6. [4]

HM Treasury (2020), *Magenta Book: Central Government guidance on evaluation*, https://www.gov.uk/government/publications/the-magenta-book. [37]

HM Treasury (2020), *The Green Book: appraisal and evaluation in central government*, https://www.gov.uk/government/publications/the-green-book-appraisal-and-evaluation-in-central-governent. [33]

Høeberg, L. et al. (2011), *Evaluering Unge-Godt i gang*, Danish Agency for Labour Market and Recruitment, https://star.dk/om-styrelsen/publikationer/2011/06/evaluering-unge-godt-i-gang/. [18]

Iacus, S., G. King and G. Porro (2012), "Matching for Causal Inference Without Balance Checking", *SSRN Electronic Journal*, https://doi.org/10.2139/SSRN.1152391. [9]

Kauhanen, A. and H. Virtanen (2021), "Heterogeneity in Labor Market Returns to Adult Education", *ETLA Working Papers*, No. 91, http://pub.etla.fi/ETLA-Working-Papers-91.pdf. [26]

Kluve, J. and J. Stöterau (2014), *A Systematic Framework for Measuring Employment Impacts of Development Cooperation Interventions*, Deutsche Gesellschaft für Internationale Zusammenarbeit (GIZ) GmbH, https://energypedia.info/images/5/54/A_Systematic_Framework_for_Measuring_Employment_Impacts_of_Development_Cooperation_Interventions.pdf (accessed on 4 June 2020). [5]

Krogh Graversen, B., B. Damgaard and A. Rosdahl (2007), *Hurtigt I Gang*, Socialforskningsinstituttet, https://pure.vive.dk/ws/files/256773/0710_Hurtigt_i_gang.pdf. [13]

Leeuw, F. and J. Vaessen (2009), *Address the attribution problem*, Network of Networks of Impact Evaluation, http://www.dmeforpeace.org/sites/default/files/Leeuw%20and%20Vaessen_Ch4.pdf. [1]

New Zealand Treasury (2015), *Guide to Social Cost Benefit Analysis*, https://www.treasury.govt.nz/publications/guide/guide-social-cost-benefit-analysis. [34]

OECD (2022), *Impact Evaluation of Vocational Training and Employment Subsidies for the Unemployed in Lithuania*, Connecting People with Jobs, OECD Publishing, Paris, https://doi.org/10.1787/c22d68b3-en. [10]

OECD (2020), "Impact evaluation of labour market policies through the use of linked administrative data", OECD, Paris, https://www.oecd.org/els/emp/Impact_evaluation_of_LMP.pdf. [35]

OECD (2020), "Impact Evaluations Framework for the Spanish Ministry of Labour and Social Economy and Ministry of Inclusion, Social Security and Migrations", OECD, Paris, http://t4.oecd.org/els/emp/Impact_Evaluations_Framework.pdf. [3]

Rosholm, M. and M. Svarer (2009), *Kvantitativ evaluering af Alle i Gang*, Danish Agency for Labour Market and Recruitment, https://star.dk/media/1361/alle-i-gang-kvantitativ-evaluering.pdf. [14]

Rosholm, M. and M. Svarer (2009), *Kvantitativ evaluering af Hurtig i gang 2 Af*, Danish Agency for Labour Market and Recruitment, https://star.dk/media/1478/hurtigt-i-gang-2-kvantitativ-evaluering.pdf. [12]

SECO (2021), *Optimierung RAV-Beratung*, https://www.arbeit.swiss/secoalv/de/home/menue/institutionen-medien/projekte-massnahmen/rav-beratung.html. [22]

Smith, D. (2008), *Analytical Framework for the Medium Term Indicators (MTI) Framework*, Unpublished. [38]

Svarer, M. et al. (2014), *Evaluering af mentorindsats til unge uden uddannel- se og job*, Danish Agency for Labour Market and Recruitment, https://star.dk/media/6995/evaluering-mentorindsats-til-unge-uden-uddannelse-og-job.pdf. [15]

The Danish Agency for Labour Market and Recruitment (STAR) (2019), *Evidence-based policy-making*, https://www.star.dk/en/evidence-based-policy-making/.   [11]

Wooldridge, J. (2009), *Introductory econometrics : a modern approach*, South Western Cengage Learning, Mason OH.   [6]

Notes

[1] Authors calculation of appendix data from Card, Kluve and Weber (2018[7]).

[2] Lasso regression is used to determine these variables, via the minimisation of the Extended Bayesian Information Criteria.

[3] Prof. Guy Lacroix (Université Laval and HEC Montréal), Prof. Michael Lechner (University of St. Gallen, Swiss Institute for Empirical Economic Research) and Prof. Jeffrey Smith (University of Wisconsin-Madison), have all provided systematic and sustained peer review contributions to the evaluation cycles.

5 Communication and evidence-based policy making

Employment and Social Development Canada (ESDC) has committed to an open and transparent appraisal of its policies. It routinely publishes its impact assessments on the Canadian Government websites and makes efforts to present technical and non-technical summaries of its impact assessments. Evaluation is conducted separately for Provinces and Territories (PTs), enabling evaluation results to be shared that speak to local effects of active labour market policy. Working relationships with PTs developed over years of collaboration facilitate the smooth transfer of knowledge between federal and provincial government. Analytical teams make efforts to share research with external technical working groups. Minor changes to how ESDC presents the information to the public, in order to better frame key messages coming from the analysis, may help to communicate analysis even more effectively and to a broader audience.

5.1. Introduction

Clarity of communication is essential so that audiences can understand the analysis and clearly see how it influences the key questions at hand. Without a clear and articulate narrative on what the evidence shows, it is hard to effect change. Effective communication and transparency are crucial throughout the whole analytical lifecycle (OECD, 2021[1]). Communication needs to be pitched at the appropriate audience to deliver effectively the key messages. For the public this may mean simple language and representation. Whilst for an academic seminar audience a careful and detailed examination of the specifics may be required. However it is delivered, this communication is essential so that policy development and implementation makes effective use of what is known about its likely effects. This chapter briefly reviews how Employment and Social Development Canada (ESDC) disseminates and communicates the analysis its conduct.

5.2. Analytical dissemination and communication

The combination of a federal evaluation framework and work within ESDC to foster transparency, means that evaluation work programmes are well defined, clear and accountable. The federal Policy on Results, which was introduced in 2016, sets out a clear set of instructions which departments must adhere to, in order to continuously evaluate programmes. This includes obligations on evaluation frameworks, reports on programme impacts and monitoring and reporting requirements. There is also a high-level commitment within senior management in ESDC to open and transparent policy evaluation. Following a commitment by the Canadian Government to sign up to the Open Government Partnership in 2011, officials in the Evaluation Directorate in ESDC were keen for ALMPs to be an exemplar in this respect. A paper was published that set out their intended approach to evaluating ALMPs, the reasons why this approach was chosen and how lessons had been learned from previous work (Gingras et al., 2017[2]). Having a public commitment of this kind is important in establishing trust with citizens that policies will be appraised fairly and efficiently (Grimmelikhuijsen, 2012[3]; Güemes, 2019[4]). A culture of transparent policy evaluation is vital to build and embed meaningful and effective policy analysis communication within an organisation (Cairney and Kwiatkowski, 2017[5]; HM Treasury, 2020[6]).

The focus on transparent and open communication from leadership is also visible in the work that evaluation staff deliver and how they communicate externally. The evaluation team in ESDC has showcased its work at national and international conferences and meetings over the years. These presentations have covered the entirety of the work from data collation to impact analysis and looking further to the next stage of their analytical development, machine learning. The presentations continue the commitment made by the ESDC on open government and allow the team to share the knowledge that they have gained whilst gathering feedback and insights that may help their own analytical development.

Results from the evaluations are shared with the public online, via the Canada Government website. There is a publication portal that documents research reports and allows users to access analysis. The results are often published in two separate formats; a more comprehensive research report, which contains more of the details on the underlying analysis, the methodology and the results, and a shorter press-release type evaluation summary, which is mainly displayed via the website but is available as a document as well. This appeals to a fairly widespread audience and is written in a non-technical manner, such that external parties can easily assimilate the data.

Greater efforts made to proactively communicate information to the public may help to further spread information, to the media and directly to the public. It does not appear that there are widespread press releases to accompany, advertise and share evaluation results as they are published, either using the news service of the Government of Canada or on social media. ESDC press and media teams should consider how best to communicate results more widely. MDRC in the United States provides a good example of an institution that uses newsletters and its social media accounts to proactively share information on its research on social policy (MDRC, 2021[7]). Doing this has allowed to expand the reach of its work. ESDC could make better use of the news service on the Government of Canada website and reach out to its 120 000 Twitter followers, with summaries of its key evaluation results.

The location of the evaluation reports, as they are currently placed, means they are more likely to be viewed by a member of the press, or other external researcher who is specifically researching the topic. This is not a problem per se, but it does suggest that further thought could be given to how the general public could access information on how effective the Labour Market Development Agreements (LMDAs) are, with a view to encouraging participation (especially among those former employment insurance claimants, who might not have any other interaction with counselling services). A potentially helpful place to have further information on the positive effects of the LMDAs might be on the "Employment Benefits" section of the Canada Government website. This is much more likely to be the place that an unemployed jobseeker goes to for information and so could present an opportunity for information to be shared passively, without the individual actively searching for that specific information.

The evaluation summaries (for an example see ESDC (2017[8])) that are produced may also benefit from some re-organisation to make the key messages even clearer. Like the main evaluation reports, separate summaries are available for Canada and all of the separate Provinces and Territories (PTs). The key results are found halfway down the page and are rather passive, talking in general terms rather than about the impact on individuals. Terminology should be reviewed to reduce jargon. Further efforts could also be made to improve the quality of the visual information provided on the website, particularly to the infographic information displayed. It contains information that is largely extraneous to the casual observer, such as the basic description of the how the estimates are made and the spending and volume of the different programmes. The infographic is trying to simultaneously describe the programmes, how the funding delivers interventions, how the evaluation was made, and the results of that evaluation. A clearer exposition here of what purpose and for whom the communication is for would allow a better focus on how to establish the key messages. Efforts to communicate the range of possible evaluation results, building on the sensitivity analysis conducted, to more technical audiences would be helpful to a deeper discussion of the results (Manski, 2011[9]).

The Danish Agency for Labour Market and Recruitment (STAR) offers a good example of how to package often complex and detailed analysis into content that can be easily digested by audiences with differing technical abilities. Its Jobeffekter website, https://www.jobeffekter.dk/, is a knowledge bank jointly created in collaboration with independent researchers. It categorises research into easily definable groups ("Unemployed", "Vulnerable social benefits recipients", "People on sick leave"), once a group has been selected, specific interventions can be chosen (for example, "Interviews" or "Training and Education"). It then produces summary information on the number of study results in this area, assesses the strength of evidence and details a summary of the job effect (for example, "Positive", "Contradictory evidence", or "Few studies") across a range of outcome variables. This allows the reader to see at a glance the strength of evidence in an accessible and non-technical manner. Further navigation within the specific results allows the more inquisitive or expert viewer to scrutinise the studies contained within this aggregate assessment and to see how each contributes to the overall score. The presentation of information and its formatting offers some insights on how to organise information in a systematic and accessible way for individuals. For ESDC this means clearly separating out communications for different audiences, packaging information for jobseekers in a clear and compelling manner and making information accessible. ESDC working with PTs, they could jointly discuss the most appropriate way to advertise this information across Canada, via ESDC and individual PTs communication channels.

5.2.1. Communication of analytical results to PTs

The channel of communication between ESDC and the PTs is vital to the functioning of ALMPs. This communication reportedly functions very well between the evaluation directorate and the officials within the PTs responsible for ALMPs. This is a result of the structures that have been put in place and the years of relationship building as the evaluation of the LMDAs have been jointly delivered. The first stage of communications is via the ongoing communication with PTs to plan and organise the analysis. The evaluation steering group that organises this work is seen as an inclusive and nimble working-level organisation that is successful at facilitating this communication. The second iteration of LMDA evaluation has also allowed ESDC to become more responsive to policy needs at the regional level, via the improvement in delivery speed of analysis. There is a collegiate relationship between them and they state that they work well together towards common goals.

Officials with responsibility for ALMPs in the PTs are cognisant of the evidence that has been built for their area and are actively involved in the planning and delivery of the LMDA evaluation. The joint responsibility for conducting the evaluations, alongside the process for planning and agreeing the objectives for each cycle of analysis contribute to a shared sense of purpose and ownership for the work. Whilst the quantitative analytical work is centrally conducted by ESDC, the fact that each PTs get a separate personalised report for their area means that they are each able to take and communicate evidence that has been generated unique to their locality and that assesses the issues affecting their populations. Those PTs that lack their own analytical capacity to conduct rigorous evaluation of their policies have been able to communicate with ESDC and ask for extra federal analytical support for specific research questions. ESDC has been forthcoming with this help where resources allow.

Despite the efforts made to provide individual evaluation reports to the PTs, there are constraints of operating federal evaluations of regional programme, because there is less resource for detailed individual qualitative work and there are data limitations on how much the quantitative analysis can say about how the specific delivery methods in a PTs impact upon participation outcomes. Removing surveys and utilising administrative data has significantly reduced delivery costs, but has come at the expense of detailed qualitative insight into regional delivery. The recommendations stemming from each of the regional reports are largely generic and not specific to the individual region. Interviews with local officials engaged in the delivery of ALMPs are conducted and these do provide some important contextual information, but they are limited in scope (they sometimes comprise five to ten individuals only) and there is no inclusion of the views of programme participants. Because of this, it is difficult to communicate an in-depth and intuitive feeling for how the policies are delivered at a local level. For local officials though, this does not hinder their interpretation of the findings, because they have all of the information they need to make this assessment separately.

Communication functions well between federal government and the officials in provincial government who plan and deliver the LMDA. Opportunities to share best practice and learning and to build relationships in a face to face setting have been disrupted by COVID-19, the reintroduction of these will help to ensure evidence is shared and used widely among the individual PTs. Evaluations may not on their own allow external stakeholders as deep an insight into the how the programmes work. In this instance, further qualitative work, and testing using smaller-scale trials, would permit better assessment and communication of delivery and implementation methods.

5.3. Analysis and policy making cycle

Over time the delivery of high quality and robust policy evaluations has allowed evaluation officials to forge a deeper relationship with ministers and policy and programme counterparts. When the LMDA evaluations were first produced, results were just provided to ESDC policy and programme staff for them to utilise in their day-to-day policy and implementation work. Now there is greater co-working between analysts in the evaluation directorate and these policy and programme ESDC staff, which allows analysis to be fed into policy development and delivery on a more consistent and systematic basis. This helps to ensure that the narrative that is built around policy development and implementation is evidence-based. Because the evaluation directorate has been able to deliver high-quality estimates of the LMDAs and their underlying programmes, it has allowed them to build trust and forge stronger working relationships. Part of the development of a closer working relationship between evaluation analysts and programme colleagues has meant that evidence on programme effectiveness is now brought in to annual budget discussions and used by the deputy minister to defend and advocate for the policy. This shift started gradually since 2011, after the first round of LMDA evaluation results. Evaluation findings now have much greater role in informing policy recommendations. This has been built upon the successful delivery of evaluation work, which could confidently demonstrate that programmes offer value-for-money and is leveraged further by the closer working relationship between analysts and policy and programme colleagues, ensuring that analysis is now a bedrock of the policy narrative. The annual monitoring and assessment reports published by ESDC document the latest evaluation results, demonstrating how they provide value for money (ESDC, 2021[10]) and allowing the department to provide evidence of the use and value of its work to the broader public.

The Forum of Labour Market Ministers also offers an opportunity to share information to senior federal and provincial policy makers, so they can have an informed discussion on policy and delivery planning. Federal and provincial officials use this forum and the working groups associated with it to socialise results and reach consensus. Evaluation results have informed various debates at these meetings since their production.

There are several examples where the results from the impact evaluations have been directly helpful in policy discussions. Evidence on the effectiveness of the LMDAs was cited as being critical to the expansion of employment insurance eligibility in 2017. The Treasury Board approves each year the programme funding agreements and the impact evaluations undertaken by ESDC are used to support securing this funding. On the softer side, evidence is reported to be instrumental for the induction of new ministers and senior officials, as it helps to set the scene and allows officials to confidently articulate the policy and its benefits. Evidence on the timing of interventions (Handouyahia et al, 2014[11]) helped ESDC make the case to PTs about the need for timely and robust monitoring data, so that individuals could be helped swiftly back into work. This helped ESDC make the case for the need for them to receive these data from PTs so they could further develop evidence on what works. Evidence has also allowed ESDC to counter negative publicity claims, particularly when external organisations question the effectiveness of ALMPs.

But there are also some limitations on the extent to which analysis has changed policy delivery. The type of impact assessment conducted means that programme results are compared against "no programme". In reality this is unlikely to occur, as the PTs receive a set level of funding from federal government and spend this money regardless. There are not more nuanced results available, such as whether or not more intensive programmes produce better outcomes, what sort of contracting framework best incentivises private providers, or whether government deliver services better than private providers. These second level of questions may be of greater use in altering how ALMPs are actually delivered by PTs. A graphical inspection of Figure 2.3 does not suggest any great shift in the proportional mix of programme type, after wave two evaluation results were delivered in 2017- suggesting that PTs largely continued on as usual, even when it appeared that some policies offered vastly better value-for-money than others.

To summarise, ESDC makes concerted efforts to share the results of its evaluation work with external stakeholders. The legislative framework that mandates cyclical evaluation of the LMDAs helps to provide a bedrock for openness, and has been taken up by senior management within ESDC to commit to a transparent analytical work programme. This provides assistance across several domains. It helps to set the tone for collaborative working with PTs, it provides encouragement to evaluation analysts to disseminate and share their work with external experts and researchers, and it helps to broaden the reach of analysis within ESDC by facilitating the development of working relationships with policy and programme colleagues. This work could be further built upon by reviewing the content and delivery of key messages to different external audiences to improve the understanding of the evaluation results, particularly among the general public.

References

Cairney, P. and R. Kwiatkowski (2017), "How to communicate effectively with policymakers: combine insights from psychology and policy studies", *Palgrave Commun 3*, Vol. 3/37, https://doi.org/10.1057/s41599-017-0046-8.

[5]

ESDC (2021), *2019/2020 Employment Insurance Monitoring and Assessment Report*, Employment and Social Development Canada, http://www12.esdc.gc.ca/sgpe-pmps/p.5bd.2t.1.3ls@-eng.jsp?pid=72896.

[10]

ESDC (2017), *2012-2017 Evaluation of the Labour Market Development Agreements Evaluation Summary*, Employment and Social Development Canada, https://www.canada.ca/en/employment-social-development/corporate/reports/evaluations/labour-market-development-agreements/summary.html.

[8]

Gingras, Y. et al. (2017), "Making Evaluation More Responsive to Policy Needs: The Case of the Labour Market Development Agreements", *Canadian Journal of Program Evaluation*, Vol. 32/2, https://doi.org/10.3138/cjpe.31119.

[2]

Grimmelikhuijsen, S. (2012), "Linking transparency, knowledge and citizen trust in government: An experiment", *International Review of Administrative Sciences*, Vol. 78/1, pp. 50-73, https://doi.org/10.1177/0020852311429667.

[3]

Güemes, C. (2019), ""Wish you were here" confianza en la administración pública en Latinoamérica", *Revista de Administração Pública*, Vol. 53/6, pp. 1067-1090, https://doi.org/10.1590/0034-761220180230.

[4]

Handouyahia et al (2014), *Effects of the timing of participation in employment assistance services : technical study prepared under the second cycle for the evaluation of the labour market development agreements*, Employment and Social Development Canada, https://publications.gc.ca/site/eng/9.834560/publication.html.

[11]

HM Treasury (2020), *Magenta Book: Central Government guidance on evaluation*, https://www.gov.uk/government/publications/the-magenta-book.

[6]

Manski, C. (2011), "Policy analysis with incredible certitude", *Economic Journal*, Vol. 121/554, https://doi.org/10.1111/J.1468-0297.2011.02457.X.

[9]

MDRC (2021), *News & Media*, https://www.mdrc.org/news/news-media.

[7]

OECD (2021), *OECD Report on Public Communication: The Global Context and the Way Forward*, OECD Publishing, Paris, https://doi.org/10.1787/22f8031c-en.

[1]

www.ingramcontent.com/pod-product-compliance
Lightning Source LLC
Chambersburg PA
CBHW082108210326
41599CB00033B/6635